Praise for *The Spa*

'If you are managing a start-up business in the creative sector this book has great guiding principles and insights. If you have been managing a creative business for some years this book will remind you of many things that ought to be on your to-do list. I'm sure I'll be dipping in and out of Greg's book for many years to come.'
David Sproxton CBE, Co-founder and Executive Chairman, Aardman Animation

'Greg is as stimulating off the page as he is in person.'
Robert Tansey, Executive Director, Sky Creative, BskyB

'Greg Orme has put his finger on the pulse of creative businesses and come up with a remarkable handbook for founders, managers and employees trying to create or recreate the type of environment they need to grow and succeed – bravo!'
John Bates, Fellow in Strategy and Entrepreneurship at London Business School

'A refreshing, honest and inspiring look at how to get the creative juices flowing within any team. Punchy, concise and tackles the thorny issues head on, with some fantastically insightful anecdotes.'
Mark Ellis, Managing Director, London-based digital agency Syzygy

This book is the most relevant and empowering book on creative leadership I have ever read – truly a great and useful inspiration for leading creative people.
Sune Roland, Head of Channels, TV 2 Networks, Denmark

'If the process of turning culture into creativity into success is something of alchemy, then Greg Orme must be a master chemist. Insightful, inspiring and practical. *The Spark* is essential reading for anyone wanting to harness that creativity to drive business success.'
Wil Harris, Head of Digital, Condé Nast UK

'How to keep the flame of creativity burning under the oxygen-depleting blankets of corporate bureaucracy is the single biggest challenge facing 21st-century managers. On the lessons drawn from his brilliantly researched case studies of companies and individuals who know how to do it, Greg Orme has assembled a master-class in creative management. Timely, important and eminently practicable, *The Spark* should be read and re-read by anyone with a stake in keeping the flame alive.'
Gordon Torr, a former Global Creative Director of global advertising agency JWT, and author of *Managing Creative People*

'At last! A book that explains the power of commercial creativity - and how it can be used to turnaround your business fortunes. Superb.'
Emyr Afan, Founder and Chief Creative Officer, Avanti Media

'*The Spark* is engaging, insightful and totally relevant. Packed with good ideas, it has a real sense of purpose and goes to the heart of what it means to manage creative people and run a creative business. The basic ideas are smart and perceptive, the examples well chosen and the layout is easy to follow all of which makes this an inspiring and genuinely useful book.'
Nick Catliff, Managing Director, Lion Television

'*The Spark* is essential reading for anyone who takes creativity in business seriously. Managing for ideas can sometimes feel like nailing jelly to a wall – but Greg Orme has managed to make it seem very achievable. He shows business insight needn't be dry and dull: this is funny, full of fantastic tips and anecdotes – and offers unique access to some great creative minds. A top book, highly recommended.'
Stuart Murphy, Director, Sky Entertainment Channels

'A must-read for anyone looking for that bolt of inspiration to boost their business. *The Spark* provides an incredibly engaging, and most importantly practical guide to ensuring any creative business is always at the very top of its game. Trying to come up with that next era-defining idea can feel like getting lost in a maze. The Spark provides a much-needed map.'
Tim Cunningham, Head of Daytime, Princess Productions

'If you run a creative business and want to take the tension out of getting the best from people – Greg Orme has written your handbook.'
Adrian Monck, Managing Director, Communications, World Economic Forum

The Spark

How to ignite and lead business creativity

Greg Orme

Ignite the Spark!

PEARSON

Harlow, England • London • New York • Boston • San Francisco • Toronto • Sydney
Auckland • Singapore • Hong Kong • Tokyo • Seoul • Taipei • New Delhi
Cape Town • São Paulo • Mexico City • Madrid • Amsterdam • Munich • Paris • Milan

Pearson Education Limited
Edinburgh Gate
Harlow CM20 2JE
United Kingdom
Tel: +44 (0)1279 623623
Web: www.pearson.com/uk

First published 2014 (print and electronic)

© Greg Orme 2014 (print and electronic)

The right of Greg Orme to be identified as author of this work has been asserted by
him in accordance with the Copyright, Designs and Patents Act 1988.

Pearson Education is not responsible for the content of third-party internet sites.

ISBN: 978-1-292-00528-7 (print)
        978-1-292-00530-0 (PDF)
        978-1-292-00531-7 (ePub)
        978-1-292-00529-4 (eText)

British Library Cataloguing-in-Publication Data
A catalogue record for the print edition is available from the British Library

Library of Congress Cataloging-in-Publication Data
Orme, Greg.
    The spark : how to ignite and lead business creativity/ Greg Orme.
        pages cm
    Includes bibliographical references and index.
    ISBN 978-1-292-00528-7 (pbk.)
    1. Creative ability in business. 2. Creative thinking. 3. Technological
innovations. 4. Diffusion of innovations. 5. New products. I. Title.
    HD53.O76 2014
    658.3'14--dc23
                                                2014010476

10 9 8 7 6 5 4 3 2 1
18 17 16 15 14

Cartoon illustrations: Bill Piggins
Cover design: Dan Mogford

Print edition typeset in 9pt Stone Serif by 30
Print edition printed and bound in Great Britain by Henry Ling Ltd., at the Dorset
Press, Dorchester, Dorset
NOTE THAT ANY PAGE CROSS REFERENCES REFER TO THE PRINT EDITION

For the sparks in my life...Gabe, Freddie & Sophie.

Contents

About the author

Greg is a consultant, coach and change agent who helps businesses to achieve transformational results. Specialising in cultures which require creativity and innovation he works with senior executives to develop inspiring leadership and drive organisational change.

Through his own business – Kirkbright – Greg works with businesses large and small. His global clients include Sky, Ogilvy & Mather, the International Olympic Committee, The World Economic Forum, Aardman Animations, Randstad Group and Virgin Media.

After gaining an MBA at London Business School, Greg became the founding CEO of the School's Centre for Creative Business. Before that he was a national journalist with ITN's award-winning Channel Five News. Greg returned to London Business School as an Associate Programme Director – as well as working as an Associate of Ashridge Business School.

Greg lives in leafy Warwickshire with his wife, two sons, a cat, four chickens and a chocolate Labrador called Rolo. You can contact him and read his blog on 'Inspiring Leadership, Strategy & Change' at http://gregorme.org/.

Publisher's acknowledgements

We are grateful to the following for permission to reproduce copyright material:

Figures

Figure 6.3 after Exhibit 1: The Ashridge Mission Model, Mission and Management Commitment, Andrew Campbell, Ashridge Strategic Management Centre, March 1996.

Text

Extract from 'If' by Rudyard Kipling from *Reward and Fairies*, published by Doubleday, reprinted by permission of United Agents on behalf of: The National Trust for Places of Historic Interest or Natural Beauty.

In some instances we have been unable to trace the owners of copyright material, and we would appreciate any information that would enable us to do so.

Author's acknowledgements

You'll read in this book that creativity is a team sport. That's what I found when writing this book.

I owe a huge debt of gratitude to all the people who have collaborated with me over the years. You're too numerous to mention individually but here are a few inspiring groups: all the people and businesses I worked with at the Centre for Creative Business at London Business School; all the clients with whom I've debated the do's and don'ts of leading commercial creativity and guiding creative businesses; and, of course, the inspiring executives who have participated so enthusiastically in my leadership and business development programmes across several continents.

Thanks to the amazing businesses around the world who've invited me in to help with strategy, leadership and change, including Sky, Ogilvy & Mather, the International Olympic Committee, Shine Group, The World Economic Forum, Syzygy, TV2, Aardman Animations, Randstad Group, Avanti Media and Virgin Media. Without you this wouldn't have been possible.

A big thank you to the generosity and insights from my brilliant interviewees including Sir John Hegarty from Bartle Bogle Hegarty; Robert Tansey, Stuart Murphy, Deborah Baker and Liz Darran from Sky; Markus Nordburg from CERN; Jeremy Shaw and Paul Kitcatt from Digitas Kitcatt Nohr; Nick Catliff from Lion Television; Wally Olins from Saffron Brand Consultants; David Sproxton CBE from Aardman Animations; Marie-Claire Barker and Nicola Ukiah from Ogilvy & Mather; Philip Chin from Langland; Richard Hytner from Saatchi & Saatchi; Stuart Cosgrove from Channel 4; and Dame Gail Rebuck from Penguin Random House.

Special thanks for your inspiration and feedback to Professor John Bates, Gordon Torr, Caroline Thompson, Dan Burman and Damian Fitzsimmons. And, of course, thanks to my insightful editor at FT Publishing, Nicole Eggleton.

Thanks to my indefatigable father, Graham, who supported me every step of the way, reading and re-reading the manuscript. Dad, you're one in a million.

Mum and 'the girls', Carol and Cheryl, thanks for your love and encouragement, always.

And my heartfelt thanks and eternal gratitude to my wonderful supportive wife Sophie, and very special boys Freddie and Gabriel. Thanks for putting up with my weekend absences from family life as I holed up in my upstairs office tap-tap-tapping away.

Introduction: The Spark

"We only get a spark when the stone and the flint are moving in opposite directions."
Traditional saying

Have you ever walked into a business and sensed something special in the air? A glint in the eye of people you meet that speaks volumes about their passion for the job and the company they're working for. A spark of playfulness, curiosity and potential. An exciting static charge of courageous creativity. Is that kind of energy pulsing through your business?

This book is about how to lead an organisation, department or team in which creativity and innovation flourish. Accelerating global competition, disruptive technology and radical changes to employee expectations mean a creative culture is no longer a 'nice-to-have'. To dodge these commercial bullets, your business must be able to keep and deliver new ideas. Fast.

Innovation is business-critical because creative companies make more money. A burning passion to improve things – to make a difference to the world – is no longer an adornment to the usual success factors: reliable delivery, high productivity and outstanding service. If efficiency and execution are this year's profits; next year's profits – and the years after that – are driven by creativity and new ideas.

In over 20 years of working with creative businesses, I've been privileged to experience an exciting energy in those studios, offices and meeting rooms. This book explores the crackling electricity in truly creative companies, I call it **The Spark:**

- **The Spark** is the potential for creativity in a person, a team – or a whole business.

- **The Spark** is a great idea that changes perceptions, drives innovation **and** makes money.

My mission is to offer you a practical tool kit to develop a charged climate in your team or business. To make sparks commonplace so your organisation can innovate successfully in a fast-changing commercial world. This book demystifies the leadership and management habits needed to turn up the power supply: to create sparks in you, your team and your business.

What do creative industries have to teach the rest of the business world?

Without a creative culture, innovation doesn't happen. After all, the basis for what are known in the corporate world as ideas pipelines, innovation programmes or even, rather grandly, Ideas Olympics – where ideas are judged, green lit and then commercialised – makes one important assumption: the business has a steady stream of new ideas in the first place. Sadly, this is rarely the case. A creative climate encourages creativity in people, which encourages new ideas. If innovation is the newborn chick, a creative culture is the egg.

From whom should we learn? Who does this stuff for their 'day job'? Who are the best people on the planet at leading commercial creativity? The answer, of course, is the creative industries themselves: content businesses in TV, film, games, music and publishing; and creative service businesses like advertising agencies. We start here because these types of businesses are built to be ideas factories. It's in their DNA. For them the urgent requirement for a constant stream of new ideas to cope with a changing world is not new. It's always been the reality – the core of what they are about. At their best, these non-hierarchical, irreverent and entrepreneurial companies provide invaluable lessons in combining creativity and commercial success. Over the years I've analysed the unique, and often counterintuitive, aspects of running a creative business that's worth shouting from the rooftops to the rest of the business world. In this book I'll share them with you.

We'll start with the creative industries, but not stop there. I've been inspired by the manufacturers of washing powder and mobile phones and the scientists exploring the secrets of the Big Bang, amongst many others. I've always felt the term 'creative industries' is a useful collective noun for governments and academics to bandy about – but a tad ludicrous and not a little presumptuous. Creativity can, and should, crop up in all types of business. This book reveals the secrets of the most inspiring companies in the world to the benefit of leaders everywhere.

Who is this book for?

The standard management model is broken. Management was never easy. But now it's like being stuck on a treadmill, blindfold, where the 'go faster' button has been taped down. In the face of a post-financial crash environment – where dizzying change is the only constant – old-style management simply is unable to respond. It still seeks consistency as an outcome. But business now needs fast, flexible solutions, highly collaborative teams and fresh approaches to succeed.

Creativity is the solution because it's all about accepting and embracing unexpected outcomes. This book is intended as a lifeline for anyone in a leadership or management position by accident or design. It argues that leaders can't make it alone: they need support and engagement from their people like never before. It also asserts that organisations desperately need to be more innovative, inspiring and meaningful places to work – simply to survive. It's for anyone who is in a leadership or management role within a business that needs to be creative and innovative – here are a few scenarios.

Business level

■ **I run an 'ideas business'**: A time-honoured route to importing some new ideas and creativity into a business is to acquire smaller, entrepreneurial businesses. This approach has wasted oceans of money for many because the issue of leading a combined creative culture was not addressed. This book offers a route to achieving the same ends more cheaply and permanently. It will help leaders who want to learn about creative business leadership that can be applied with their own people – in a team – or across the whole of their organisation. It will be useful for sectors whose survival depends on the constant flow of new ideas: fast-moving consumer goods, retailing, technology, leisure and pharmaceutical industries, to name a few.

- **I run a people business:** A creative business is the ultimate people business. This book is for industries where people, knowledge and the application of expertise are key success drivers: law and accounting partnerships, consultancies of many colours, recruitment and software design businesses, for example.

- **I run a creative industry business:** A sizeable proportion of my consulting life has been with the founders, directors and senior executives of nimble, independent creative businesses in the digital, TV, games, film, publishing and marketing spheres. They are already very creative, and want to stay that way. They may have created an ideas factory but are not sure what the exact formula was – and how to sustain it. This book is a golden opportunity to reflect on what's working, and what's not, as well as to learn from best practice outside your business.

Team level

- **I run a creative hotspot within a larger business:** This book is especially for those charged with managing well-known creative 'hotspots' in marketing, communications, branding, sales, product design and research and development. Often businesses identify areas where creativity is required and then outsource it, or work in partnership with a creative agency. This book will help those parts of the business charged with creativity to get better results. It is a way of inviting a nonconformist and slightly anarchic, ideas-fuelled culture **inside** your team.

■ **I run a team or department that needs to be more innovative**: If you are managing a group of people that traditionally are not seen as creative – IT, HR, finance, production or sales teams, for example – this book offers some practical management tips to develop a more creative and innovative mindset.

Creative industries are not a paragon of virtue

I'm not a totally wide-eyed cheerleader for the creative industries. Many smaller creative businesses need more skilful management, more commercial acumen – and fatter margins. Meanwhile, some of the larger corporate creative organisations mentioned in these pages, like BBC, Disney and Electronic Arts, have their critics, detractors and scandals, just like any other industry. Finally, you only have to look at some truly terrible, derivative films, music and TV shows to know these businesses don't always get it right. I had to sit through *Garfield 2* (20th Century Fox) with my five-year-old son in 2007, an experience I am still trying to forget. But, when they do get it right, there is none better at building greenhouses in which the tender greens shoots of talent and ideas can intertwine and grow.

Action-orientated design

I have written with my clients in mind. They always ask for advice that can lead to action. They want practical things to **do** to develop their leadership style or improve their business. And they are always short of time. To help fit in with your hectic schedule, I have edited the chapters so they can be accommodated into snatched air and rail journeys. At the end of each short section you'll find a tip, key question or management action for you to pursue, clearly marked with the following 'Spark' icon: ☀

At the end of each chapter, you'll find a summary of the main points and a plan of action designed into my CLEAR change model.

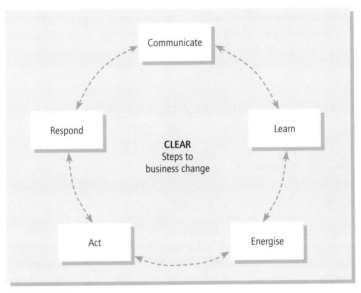

CLEAR change model

The CLEAR steps are as follows:

Step	Description
Communicate	To gather information, to listen, to collaborate. Because this is a book about leadership and management you should seek to talk things through and gather feedback throughout all the steps.
Learn	To think, to change your attitude, to diagnose.
Energise	To design, to set targets, to create.
Act	To implement, to break the rules, to create new guidelines.
Respond	To rate the impact of change, to tweak, to go back to the drawing board if need be.

Book structure

Business creativity is full of intriguing tensions. I have addressed the key questions in running a creative business or team. The structure is deliberately simple in order to help you to extract the maximum number of practical insights – and a clear 'to do' list. I've also written a short chapter at the end of the book dealing with the popular myths that surround commercial creativity.

The 10 habits

The 10 habits are numbered and will have a big impact if you approach them sequentially as you read. The chapters aimed at your managerial approach and attitudes are grouped at the beginning for a good reason. Any change to your business or team has to be led by your behaviour. But they also work together interdependently. Then they become more than the sum of the parts so, to truly transform your business, practise all 10 habits together over time.

The organisational and leadership habits are all linked to one of the five crucial key ingredients found within all creative businesses, in my experience:

1 The Spark
2 Passionate people
3 Inspiring philosophy
4 Energised culture
5 Collaborative teams

The Spark is that intangible energy and potential that leads to new ideas. The most direct route to encourage this is the way you interact with others. The key habit to follow is:

■ **Habit 1**: Start an electric conversation – how to create The Spark in your business.

Passionate people are the rocket fuel of any creative business. The three habits that help inspire passionate people are:

■ **Habit 2**: Break the management rules – how to become an electric manager.

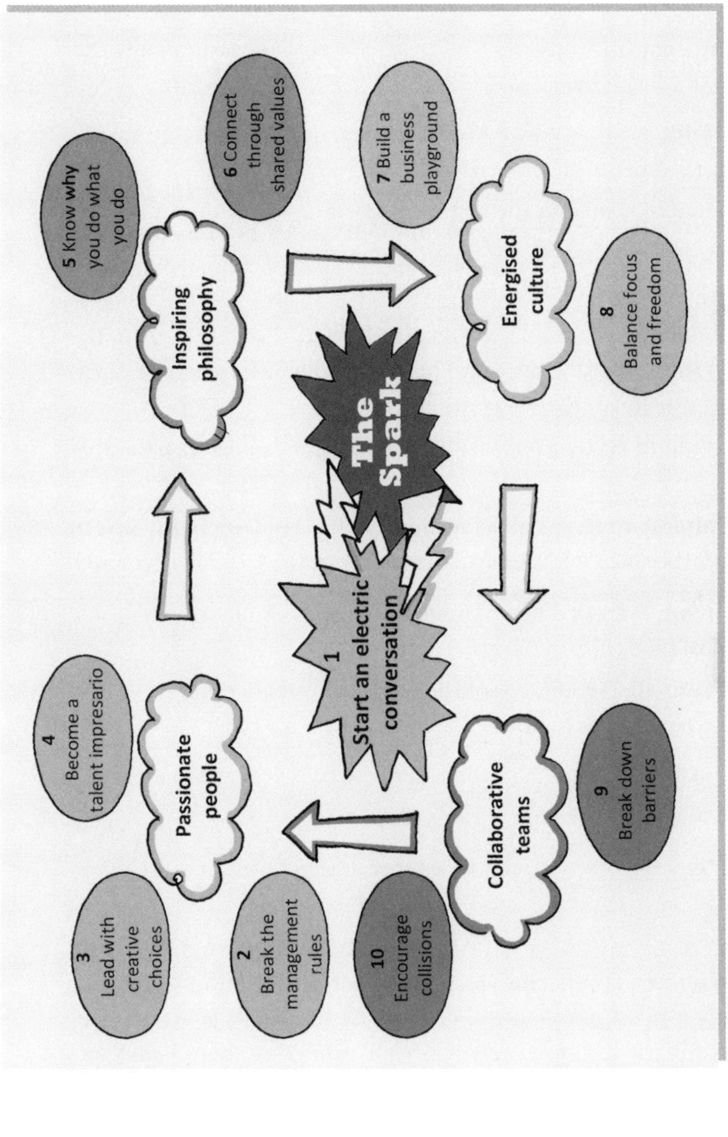

figure A.2   The five crucial key elements found within all creative businesses

- **Habit 3**: Lead with creative choices – how to choose to be an inspiring leader.

- **Habit 4**: Become a talent impresario – how to fill your business with creative talent.

Inspiring philosophy is your belief system. The twin habits that help develop it are:

- **Habit 5**: Know why you do what you do – how to find an inspiring business purpose.

- **Habit 6**: Connect through shared values – how to inspire passion in your people.

Energised culture is the weather system in which inspired people and teams work. The two habits that help make the weather are:

- **Habit 7**: Build a business playground – how to put an electric charge in your creative climate.

- **Habit 8**: Balance focus and freedom – how to manage creative tensions.

Collaborative teams make the most of scale in your business. The habits that promote creative teamwork are:

- **Habit 9**: Break down barriers – how to dynamite the walls that block creativity.

- **Habit 10**: Encourage collisions – how to spark electric conversations to power collaboration.

Be creative with these habits

"Too many rules will stifle innovation."
Sergey Brin, *co-founder*, Google[1]

If the structure above sounds straightforward – a simple 'paint by numbers' approach to changing your organisation – I have an admission: it's not. You will need to use the habits to ensure they work for you and your team, as well as making them your own. Creative leaders and managers are fearlessly independent. Use the habits in the book by all means, they work. But find your own unique way of putting them into practice. Let's get started.

Start an electric conversation
How to create The Spark in your business

You'll learn:

How to spot an electric conversation

How to start an electric conversation

The crucial role of electric conversations in creating The Spark

"Creativity is contagious, pass it on."
Albert Einstein, physicist[1]

In 1999 the whisky brand Johnny Walker was in decline. It challenged the advertising agency Bartle Bogle Hegarty (BBH) to come up with a novel way to sell its product. It wanted to develop an enduring brand idea that could transcend borders and adapt to local as well as global markets. At that point in time any campaign about whisky always featured two schools of clichéd imagery: either traditional 'heather 'n' kilts' to represent Scottish heritage or the conceit that 'whisky = success' rammed home by footage of successful businessmen sipping whisky while staring into the middle distance on the back of a yacht.

BBH realised Johnny Walker desperately needed a new, more youthful group of customers. Research into the attitudes of younger consumers sparked some **electric conversations**. From these a big idea came forth. They discovered younger people had shifted in their view of success. For them success is not a place, it's a journey – you never arrive. From the universal idea of personal progress, the 'Keep Walking' solution was born: the award-winning campaign featuring down-to-earth personal progress stories of younger people. It's since been adopted by 120 countries. Meanwhile, Johnnie Walker's value and volume sales have risen 48 per cent and 94 per cent respectively, as the whisky market has declined by 8 per cent. The campaign has helped deliver over $2.2 billion in retail sales and is still being evolved into new reincarnations by the BBH team. BBH's founder and creative director, Sir John Hegarty, told me: 'That's how intelligence, insight and strategy gives you the confidence to jump further with an idea – it leads you to better creative execution.'

Bottled lightning

Creativity is the electric moment when one person illuminates his or her consciousness with the spark of a new idea. A spark can happen when two or more people collide in a creative way. In a business, most sparks fizzle out quickly for good or bad reasons. Good reason: the sparks are judged correctly not to be strong or bright enough. Bad reason: a clumsy, neglectful or actively hostile environment to any idea which challenges the status quo.

A small number of ideas are so strong they survive and grow to become bolts of lightning that attract attention across the business. Still fewer go on to become highly profitable. Some even change the world. That's innovation: the sparks that grow into bolts of lightning that, against the odds, are bottled by a business.

Creativity – transforming the cash spent on salaries into ideas; and innovation – turning those ideas back into cash, is the Holy Grail of business.[2] Making it happen is tricky. To be skilled at facilitating commercial creativity is, arguably, the most difficult leadership role of all. But it's also one of the most valuable and rewarding things to do. Following the habits in this book will make it easier.

You can't predict lightning

Lightning is one of the oldest observed natural phenomena on Earth. It's a huge spark of static electricity – the kind that sometimes shocks you when you touch a doorknob. It's surprisingly common. About a hundred bolts strike the Earth's surface every second – and their power is extraordinary. Each bolt contains up to one billion volts of electricity. Like human inspiration, it's not possible to predict when and where lightning will strike. But we do know a lot about the unique atmospheric conditions in which lightning is more likely to strike.

Managing for creativity is the same. You can't mandate creativity, or the mix of skills and attitudes that produces it. Demanding that people are creative to order is a little bit like someone shushing a crowd of people, turning to you in the pregnant silence that ensues, and saying: 'Go on, do that funny thing you do!' In 1991, an American girlfriend actually did this to me in front of a group of friends she wanted to impress in the United States. I can assure you, the result was not amusing for anyone. Mine was a spark of humour, not a bolt of lightning, and should never have been subjected to public scrutiny. Trying to manage spontaneous humour, creativity or, indeed, lightning is awkward, difficult and prone to failure if the atmosphere is not right. So, if creativity can't be mandated, what can you do?

You can't order people to be creative any more than you can order people to be happy, fascinated or in love. But you can lead a business culture which, like the charged atmosphere in a thunder storm, produces the lightning strike of ideas. My ten organisational and leadership habits create the organisational energy for The Spark to happen - week in, week out.

☀ Leaders inspire creativity when they strike up electric conversations.

How to kick start an electric conversation

Do you know that rare and special moment when you see, hear or feel something so exciting that the hairs on the back of your neck stand on end? It might be an image you've just seen, or a discussion that overflows with excitement – so much so it's taken on an interesting life of its own. You lose track of time and become completely engrossed with the subject at hand. It feels like you've received an invitation to join an intriguing journey that might lead to a fleeting glimpse of clarity – or an even more interesting question.

That's what an electric conversation feels like.

For a moment, reflect on the most important milestones in your life: a career move, a new relationship, a big idea, getting involved with some volunteer work or a completely new direction. Chances are it began with an electric conversation with a friend, family member or collaborator. The genesis of your greatest achievements will have occurred in an instant when an idea rose unexpectedly to the surface of your consciousness and grabbed you firmly by the scruff of the neck. This catalysing insight will have led you to something truly amazing. Most people will recognise these conversations from some time in their life. Fewer people experience it at work because, in business, electric conversations are killed more often than encouraged.

It is these inspiring, direction-making, profit-creating conversations that this book is about. Electric conversations lead to the lightning strike of new ideas. They are the smallest building block of the creative business. They happen in an instant, or over years; between just two people, or a whole team. Whatever the circumstance, electric conversations drive change. They change the direction of your life – and the lives of people around you. From a business perspective, they couldn't be more important; they are behind every profit-making business idea in human history.

Electric conversations help companies benefit from scale. One person alone in a garden shed might do brilliant things. But a business has an advantage over that lone inventor – it has more people. Creative businesses are complicated and simple, all at the same time. Simple, because in essence, they are purely a number of talented people coming together supported by investment to pursue certain goals. They are complicated because of the inherent challenges in generating the conditions in which creative alchemy occurs. This book illuminates the path to developing an energised culture through passionate people, collaborative teams and the power of electric conversations.*

Different businesses in different industries will need differing levels of creativity – and a different emphasis on creativity in their organisation. You can see from Figure 1.1 how the elements of passionate people, energised culture and collaborative teams build towards a situation in which electric conversations are happening right across your business.

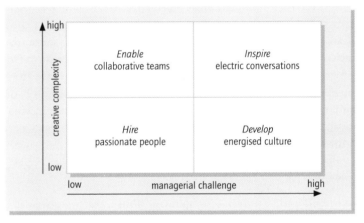

| **figure 1.1** | **Electric conversations** Source: Professor John Bates, London Business School, who emailed me a version of this 2 × 2 model after we discussed *The Spark*, December 2013 |

I'd advise any business in the world to make the effort to go the whole nine yards and lead your team to encourage electric conversations in the top right-hand box. The transformation of your business will be more than worth the managerial effort.

☀ **Use The Spark to focus upon the top priority in your business to encourage more electric conversations. The best route for you might be changes to your management style, more passion.**

* Source: Professor John Bates, London Business School

and energy in your team – or the need for a more collaborative attitude. Whatever it is, use *The Spark's* structured approach as a catalyst for beneficial change.

Inspiring collisions

It's worth setting the boundaries of what electric conversations can achieve because they are not the idea itself – or business innovation in its entirety. They are the road towards these things. It might take months for great ideas to emerge from electric conversations. They also don't negate the importance of individual flashes of brilliance. Psychological research shows people have a lot of great ideas when they are alone in what scientists call a state of 'low cortical arousal' (the rest of us call it day dreaming). In other words: you have ideas when you're not trying to. When I ask executives on the leadership development programmes I deliver around the world when and where they have their 'aha! moments' they often reply: 'In the shower' or 'at the gym' or 'walking my dog.' These are the few times in busy modern lives when we have precious minutes to switch off and allow our brains to give us some creative feedback.

Electric conversations play a part in these lonely moments of insight. This is because all of our ideas come from a magical and unique blend of external influences: books, poems, speeches, films, inspirational thinkers and leaders. We learn through day-to-day collisions with new stories, information and ideas. Your inspiration is as unique as you are: the director Woody Allen is inspired by New York City; the award-winning novelist Hilary Mantel by the Tudor period in England's history; I'm often inspired by food, chefs and great restaurants. Electric conversations are a fundamental way for businesses to encourage employees to collide with new ideas: the only way to ensure their company's knowledge gets around – and adds up to more than the sum of the parts.

※ What inspires you? How can you bring that inspiration into the office every morning?

Electric conversations and flow

Electric conversations make you happy. A Hungarian psychologist, Mihaly Csikszentmihalyi (in case you were wondering, you pronounce it: 'Me-hi Chicksent-me-hiee'), resolved to try to find out what made people happy. First, he interviewed hundreds of artists, athletes, musicians, chess masters and surgeons and asked how they felt when they were engaged in their specialist calling. He then arranged for thousands of ordinary people to wear a pager and describe how they were feeling, and what they were doing, when the pager went off randomly throughout the day.[3] (A pager, you ask? Well, it was the eighties.)

From this research, Csikszentmihalyi developed an optimal state of being he called 'flow'. When people are in flow they are so involved with an activity that nothing else seems to matter; the experience is so enjoyable they will do it even at a great cost, for the sheer sake of doing it. Flow is about joy, creativity and total involvement; a place where problems disappear and there is an exhilarating feeling of transcendence. Athletes call it 'being in the zone'; artists have described it as 'rapture'; and some mystics talk of 'ecstasy'. Electric conversation is about more than one person getting into a flow state **together**. For business leaders, the big insight is this: people will seek out electric conversations because they're enjoyable – not because they're being paid.

※ What gets you into a state of flow? It might be reading, skiing, sailing, playing chess, throwing a frisbee, talking with friends in the pub, yoga, writing, drawing, to name but a few. To understand flow at a personal level, remember that feeling. Then you'll be able to recognise when it's happening at work – and try to make it happen more often.

Key characteristics of electric conversations

Electric conversations are one key way that a business can ensure its employees are providing each other with a steady stream of ideas, inspiration and challenge. They are as much about energy, emotion and raw passion as intellectual stimulus. Sometimes they even provoke a physical sensation not unlike a small electric charge: the hairs on the back of your neck literally stand on end. That's why you need to listen carefully to your own instinct to know when an electric conversation has begun. Figure 1.2 shows six basic characteristics of an electric conversation so that you can try to have more of them – and recognise them when they start.

Idea-driven	Brave	Passionate	Playful	Purposeful	Informal
Not focused on hierarchy or competing agendas – all about the power of ideas	Constructive conflict is part of it – and potential failure takes courage	It's not possible to be collaborative and creative without caring deeply about the outcome	No assumption of 'right way'. Best when unpredictable, playful and even fun	Often happen when people share goals, values and an inspiring purpose	Can happen any time, anywhere with a colleague, the boss, a client, a supplier – and even a competitor

figure 1.2   Six key characteristics of an electric conversation

High-voltage examples

Research shows that jazz ensembles, improvised comedy and theatre troupes use versions of electric conversations to produce magical performances without a pre-prepared script.[4] We can also look to recent history for some compelling examples of electric conversations:

- John Lennon and Paul McCartney of The Beatles are one of the best-known and most successful musical collaborations in history. Between 1962 and 1969 the partnership published approximately 180 songs. Early on they would collaborate extensively when writing songs working 'eyeball to eyeball' – the ultimate musical conversation. Later, when the joint electricity faded a little, they worked alone but still published the material under the legendary team name: Lennon & McCartney.

■ Scientists Francis Crick and James Watson conducted a world-changing electric conversation at Cambridge University, investigating the fundamental building blocks of life. Famously, they often retreated to the local pub – The Eagle – to continue their discussions. One lunchtime in February 1953 Crick interrupted pub patrons to announce that they had 'discovered the secret of life'. Nine years later, the duo were awarded the Nobel Prize in Medicine for their discovery of the structure of DNA – recognised as one of the most significant scientific discoveries of the 20th century.

■ Sometimes electric conversations are inspired by necessity. In 1970 a NASA ground crew conducted one under a global spotlight and intense pressure. James Lovell, the commander of the spacecraft Apollo 13, uttered the immortal line over the intercom: 'Houston, we have a problem.' An oxygen tank had exploded, stranding the spacecraft hundreds of thousands of miles from Earth. Flight director Gene Kranz challenged ground controllers to do the impossible: to use their ingenuity to somehow help bring the astronauts home safely. Apollo 13 splashed down safely four days later.

☀ 15 Minute Experiment. Start an electric conversation today. What's the worst that can happen? You have a normal conversation. What's the best that can happen? You dream up a new idea that changes your business – or your life – for the better.

Electric conclusion

Leading commercial creativity can seem daunting. This is because it requires a number of interdependent approaches described by the habits in this book. But it helps to realise that a large part of changing your culture is about transforming the nature of your day-to-day conversations. That's the end of the process – but it can also be the start. So, start an electric conversation, right now.

Sparks to remember

➤ You can't mandate creativity, or the mix of skills and attitudes that produces it, but you can lead a culture that encourages new ideas.

➤ Electric conversations are the smallest building block of a creative culture – they lead to the spark of inspiration.

➤ Electric conversations not only drive change and profits, they inspire you – and even make you happy.

CLEAR steps to change

Communicate

Start an electric conversation today. Think of the most important question facing your business, the thing that makes you scared and hopeful all at the same time. Invite a hand-picked group of people to a no-holds barred creative conversation. Use Figure 1.2 to guide your approach. This is a golden opportunity for you to show those around you what an electric conversation should look, sound and feel like. Remember to listen more than you speak, to facilitate a flowing discussion where all are involved, and to summarise what was achieved.

Learn

Think about the most electric, idea-laden conversation you ever had in your life. What was the context and conditions that made it possible? How can you recreate that with the people around you? Grab a blank sheet of paper and brainstorm some things guaranteed to kill electric conversations in your team – anything from 'too much hierarchy' to 'room too stuffy'. Then write down the opposite – the conditions that seem to encourage them. Narrow down your list to the three things on each side of the sheet that you can do something about – then make the changes required.

Energise

Where in your team or business are electric conversations needed most? Is it in your regular weekly management meeting or a monthly board 'strategy' meeting? Perhaps, if your business is cyclical, it is in a certain time period in your calendar year – or when your team is developing ideas for a new product or client pitch? Or, are electric conversations urgently needed in after-project or pitch review sessions to improve how you do things in the future? Whenever it is for your business or team, focus on when and where the electric conversations need to take place and how you can help to start them.

Act

Think about how you can redesign a meeting to encourage more electric conversations. Are there any guidelines for how your most important regular meetings are facilitated? Can you encourage people to focus the 'big question' or hoped-for outcome of your regular management meeting to encourage a more free-flowing and inspiring debate? Right now, who talks the most and who says nothing? How can you encourage more participation through the group? Who is not invited that might come along in the future on a temporary or permanent basis to shake things up a little?

Respond

Change the game in your regular management meetings for one month and then review if things improved. Ask the members in the group individually: What worked? What didn't work? What still needs to be done? Reset and make any changes needed for another month until your management meetings are crackling with energy – rather than being a chore to be avoided.

2

Break the management rules
How to become an electric manager

You'll learn:

- Why traditional, 'one-best-way' management kills creativity
- How to avoid the hidden obstacles to creative management
- How to break the management rules – to become an electric manager
- How to design and manage your own creative process
- How to demystify where ideas come from – and use psychology to your advantage

"If new ideas are the lifeblood of any thriving organisation – and, trust me, they are – managers must learn to revere, not merely tolerate, the people who come up with those ideas."
Mark McCormack, founder of the Global Sports Management Agency, IMG[1]

When Stuart Murphy was drafted into the satellite pay TV business Sky in 2010, as director of entertainment channels, his mission was to develop and commission hit shows. One of his first challenges was to explain to the rest of the business – people who looked after the technology platform, managed engineers or oversaw call centre operatives – how the creative process is managed.

'There is something a bit Wizard of Oz about creativity,' he said.'
There's a perception it just happens mysteriously in the bath
– the famous Eureka moment. Then that lucky person goes off
the next day to make £5 trillion. In my experience, the creative
process doesn't work like that. What happens is this: there
are a few different conversations swilling around the business
on different subjects: you might be thinking about what the
customer wants; a big trend in society or an interesting new
technology. Then somebody says something and – bam! – a
bunch of previously disparate ideas coalesce around a single
idea. Then a champion semi-bulldozes through the idea bringing
fans along the way.'

To help people understand this unpredictable, conversation-
based process, Stuart now presents an update at Sky's six-
monthly senior management get-togethers. 'Instead of saying, at
the end of the process, "Ta-da! Here's the final show!", we share
the thinking process along the way. We're honest about how we
come up with new ideas. We pull the curtain back on The Wizard
of Oz.'[2]

☀ An important part of the role of manager in a
creative business is to demystify and explain the
creative process.

Why 'one-best-way' management kills creativity

Management feels like it has been around forever. But it hasn't
at all. It was invented by a man three years before the start
of the First World War. A fastidious American engineer from
Philadelphia, called Frederick Winslow Taylor, set out with his
trusty slide rule to inject a little science into the tricky art of
people management. In 1911, Taylor wrote his philosophy down
in a grand treatise called *The Principles of Scientific Management*. It
addressed a pressing challenge of the industrial era: how to mass
produce everything from cookers to clothing. His solution was to

develop 'one-best-way' for every task – from loading pig iron to packing boxes. His objective was to assign each worker a carefully designed task that could be repeated endlessly and faultlessly. Taylor's thinking leads to the design of a job down to the last placement of a spanner on a bench: the Holy Grail of consistent results, very fast, very cheap. It's a dream in which every worker bee performs to the limits of human productivity for every hour of his or her working life.

This rigid job conformity worked spectacularly well for quite a while. It was the foundation stone upon which the assembly line was built. Asking human beings to stay in one place to carry out a repetitive task whilst widgets streamed past didn't work just for Henry Ford and his iconic Model T Ford; Taylor's one-best-way did the trick for mass production of all kinds.[3] In fact, without scientific management, our great-grandparents wouldn't have benefited from cheap meat, refrigerators and carpets, amongst many other things. One-best-way lowered the cost of production and brought a whole new lifestyle within the grasp of the middle classes.

But there's a problem. Like all innovations, management should evolve to stay relevant. But it hasn't. Or, at least, not enough. One-best-way is not fit for purpose in a business environment where needs people to be creative. Of course, we need efficiency and productivity in business. But, encouraging people to be creative, inventive and innovative is at the other end of the spectrum to one-best-way. Businesses and teams that rely on creativity need lots of different ways; otherwise you don't produce lots of different outcomes.

To manage creativity you need to be aware of Taylor's ghost, which stills haunts modern boardrooms and offices. The problem is the intent behind it. Taylor may have spent a lifetime studying human productivity, but he didn't have a lot of time for your average working Joe. He once described the sort of man suited to loading pig iron as: 'so stupid and phlegmatic that he nearly resembles in his makeup the ox'. Taylor wanted management to be a 'true science, resting upon clearly defined laws, rules, and principles'.[4] Scientific management thinks of people as resources. Humans, in other words, are like oil, coal or paper clips: a resource to be used up.

Now, there's been a debate raging between the 'numbers people' and the 'people people' for hundreds of years about what really matters in business. Of course, there is a place for rote systems and processes in some roles and teams: sales, production and customer service, for example. But, let me be clear: the people who work in creative businesses and job roles are not impressed one little bit by time and motion studies that reduce their contribution to something that can be codified, prescribed, scripted to the last dotted 'i' and crossed 't'. Their educational background and expectations of work and life markedly differ from an early 20th-century labourer sweating over pig iron. Frederick Winslow Taylor would be spinning in his grave.

※ Be honest. How much of your management style is based on the idea that the people reporting to you should follow your one-best-way? Before dictating, pause and ask their opinion to see if there's a better way.

But...creative businesses do need management

At the end of the last century, Robert Sutton, a professor of management science and engineering at Stanford University, in California, set out to study the management of creativity in business. After a decade of analysis he wrote in a rather exasperated way: 'After studying creative companies and teams for more than a decade, I've found them to be remarkably inefficient and often terribly annoying places to work, where "managing by getting out of the way" is often the best approach of all.'[5]

Sutton essentially was arguing that you can't manage creativity; you can only manage **for** creativity. At a business level this is true. Creativity bubbles up from the right culture. But employees need to know where they stand. 'Getting out of the way' is not always possible, or practical. People need to know what projects they are assigned to, how long they've got, and what the objectives are. You do need some predictability and consistency: time sheets completed, services delivered to deadline, the same accounting practices, and consistent employee behaviours linked to the company's overall values. Complete hands-off management does not work, and is not reflected in the 'creative industries' themselves. Any business, however creative, has budgets, deadlines, objectives and pressing customer needs. All businesses, even creative ones, need management.

So, while I'm happy to help throw scientific management out of the office window, it needs to be replaced with something. Electric management is a fresh approach: it breaks the rules by its intent to empower people. It is the only way to run a business that offers products or services that require creativity, knowledge and expertise. Before I offer you my manifesto for electric management, let's take a whistle-stop tour of the challenges you'll face.

The challenges of managing business creativity

Before you start breaking the rules of management, there are a few challenges to be aware of.

Are you an accidental manager?

Management is talked about often in creative businesses as a 'necessary evil' – by employees, and sometimes managers, too. This is because the world is full of accidental managers. A role on the management team is seen as the logical next step for people who have excelled. Talented people are promoted, sometimes against their wishes, to a managerial post with little guidance. Usually they've picked up the art of management from odd snippets of TV, films and examples of sometimes terrible management in their own careers. As a result, some default to an inconsistent, occasionally dictatorial, impression of what they think management should be. Or, they trend the other way: they're everyone's 'best friend' and are perceived as a useless pushover. It's 'The Peter Principle', which states we'll be promoted to the level of our incompetence. Of course, this is a disaster for the person being promoted. It's also damaging for the company: 'old-style' management in a creative business is like fixing a delicate circuit board with a hammer.

But, if either of the descriptions above describes you, relax. You're not alone. I've discovered through running management development programmes for many years that very few people are born as effective and enthusiastic managers. Use this book as inspiration to design your own learning journey to make it a bit easier and more fun. Management isn't necessarily always unpleasant or difficult – it can be a rewarding adventure.

☀ Are you an accidental manager? If so use *The Spark* to develop your own more effective and personalised management approach.

Why many businesses avoid being creative – most of the time

One reason managing for creativity is tricky is it's not what most businesses are doing, most of the time. Businesses are often trying to exploit well-trodden processes and proven products to make money right now, this month, this year.

Even a creative business like Disney isn't trying to be creative all the time. A good example is how Disney manages its global theme parks in comparison with how it runs its research and development teams in Burbank, California. Theme park cast members, as they are called, follow strict rules and 'scripting', whether they are playing Mickey Mouse, a Caribbean Pirate or Goofy. Deviation from character is frowned upon. This is because Disney executives want the customer experience to be the same high standard in any one of its theme parks whether in Florida, Paris or Tokyo. However, the 'imagineers' in Burbank, who are being challenged to dream up new rides, characters and storylines for the theme park experience, are not scripted. Their approach to day-to-day working life will be very different because their management challenge is the polar opposite to the theme park cast members. One is trying to capture Disney's past successes and replicate them endlessly; the other is trying to forget the past to dream up something wild and new.

☀ As a manager you need to make informed judgement calls on the balance of resources between 'doing the day job' (theme park cast member) and allowing the time and space to create the spark of new ideas (imagineer).

Creative people are hard to manage

Creative people are hard to manage because they naturally seek to 'gold plate' their work. Managed well this can lead to outstandingly satisfied customers. But a creative person's sense of purpose and passion about finding something original may lead him or her to work so long on 'getting it right' that the business makes no profit. In many creative businesses in which I have been called in to help, unprofitability has been a major issue driven by the perfectionism of creative and technical specialists. They are also hard-wired to be unimpressed by your title and authority: what you do is more important than what's written on your name tag. Finally, they're more difficult to bribe with money. Salary and bonuses mean less to them than the majority of the population because the quality of the work and their colleagues is often equally, or even more, important.

Becoming an electric manager

When Carol landed her first job in the R&B music industry in London she knew she needed to learn the art of managing creativity – and fast. A talented amateur violinist, she'd staked a lot on reinventing herself as a record producer. For 10 years she'd been a successful City lawyer; but had become disillusioned after the credit crunch scandals. She'd landed a brilliant job. The downside: failing at the high-profile and respected Art4Profit record label would be a potentially terminal start to a new career.

She soon realised there was little point in throwing her weight around. As producer – the person responsible for bringing the creative team together to deliver the record – she was clearly as much a collaborator in the creative process as someone who could crack the whip. She realised she needed to embrace the fact that a recording studio is an ambiguous environment with no clear yardstick for 'good' or 'bad' quality, clear lines of authority or hierarchical control over the end product.

For the first week she felt ineffectual and all at sea. But then she had an insight. It was true that much was out of her control – but what was in it? By posing this question one night over a glass of wine she scribbled down the following list:

- **Setting the vision and objectives**: To make sure the album is delivered on time and to the right standard. My job is to make the success criteria for the album crystal clear – and to keep everyone on track when they start to stray from this.

- **Who plays on what**: I have the power to select and influence which musicians and artists feature on which tracks – so understanding where talented people will shine, and where they will bomb, is crucial to the success of this project.

- **My managerial approach**: A democratic, listening and facilitative style seems to work best. In this way I can 'nudge' the product to something that's high quality – and also might sell some records!

Carol also had power to set deadlines. She experimented with forcing the pace of production but quickly found this was counterproductive and produced poor-quality results. She realised it was better to agree clear, reasonable deadlines from the start and allow the many different parties involved in producing a record – songwriters, publishers, artists, session musicians and personnel marketeers – space to be creative. She noticed if she allowed them a little time to mull over particular challenges they often arrived the following morning with an innovative solution.

As the months rolled by, Carol grew in confidence and proactively started to guide the creative output through ad hoc listening sessions in which the various teams she worked with played and then dissected 'bad songs' and 'good songs' to forge a common aesthetic for each album. But she was careful to allow space for the artists to experiment with their own sound and forge their unique contribution to each project.

When the final track was finished she met her former legal colleagues in the pub and tried to explain the art of creative management: 'My job is to develop a shared purpose while still letting others apply their distinctive expertise. I like to think I operate at the "centre of the storm" without being too controlling, or the focus of attention. The satisfaction comes from helping others realise their unique talents and reach a collective goal. Fingers crossed: a hit record, we'll see!'[6]

☀ List the key success factors for managing creativity in your business or team. Then underline the factors that offer you the most leverage to beneficially guide the creative process.

Breaking the rules

Electric managers have to be thoughtful, nuanced and skilful in their approach. They need to develop higher levels of empathy and self-awareness than previous managerial incarnations. As Scott Cook, the co-founder of the US software company Intuit observes: 'Traditional management prioritises projects and assigns people to them. But increasingly, managers are not the source of the idea.'[7] People placed in a managerial position need to have the capability to *choose* when to ask for consistency; and when to allow team members to get creative. Managers need to break the management rules to encourage electric conversations:

Management rule	Breaking the rule
The intention is to produce predictable, consistent results.	The intention is to deliver consistently; but managers need to check they are not inhibiting creativity.
Command-and-control approach: directions to ensure everyone in the business follows a prescribed path.	Guiding approach: support and encourage people to higher levels of awareness and responsibility for their actions.
Focus on telling: tell people exactly what to do and then monitor how they do it.	Focus on listening: clearly outline the brief, objective or mountain to climb and then listen to how the person might use their creativity to deliver.
Treat everyone exactly the same.	Observe individuals carefully and treat them how they like to be treated – and will respond to.
Focus on process and the desired result.	Offer scope to look at things in their own way.
Ask closed questions that have only three possible answers: 'yes', 'no' or 'I'm not sure'.	Ask open questions that require people to respond with full sentences – to think and to engage.

Managing the creative process

One of the key jobs for any manager in a creative business is to oversee projects; to ensure they deliver to the right standard as well as being on time and on budget. This may sound counter-intuitive, bearing in mind creative businesses generally seek to relax the 'rules'. But, whether it's a bicycle being designed, a website being built, a movie or hit record being produced, management is always required. After nearly two decades of research into creative management, US academic Teresa Amabile argued that good 'project management' is one of the most important factors for encouraging creativity in business. Here are five principles of enlightened electric management to help you to avoid killing creativity:

1 Create clear project objectives

Invest time ensuring the brief for any creative work is detailed and specific about success criteria - but not the solution itself. Counterintuitive people are more creative when they have to solve problems within clear rules and objectives. The legendary Dutch footballer Johan Cruijff first showed off his innovative 'Cruijff Turn' in the 1974 World Cup. Instead of kicking the ball, he would drag it behind his planted foot with the inside of his other foot, turn through 180 degrees, and accelerate away from the defender. Cruijff would never have come up with this creative skill unless he'd been challenged by the limitations of playing inside the pitch touchlines.

When the brief for the project has been set, move the goalposts (and the touchlines) as little as possible. Kevin Roberts, CEO of Saatchi & Saatchi, describes how his agency provides an 'elastic-sided sandbox' for employees to play in. In other words, Saatchi & Saatchi offers clear focus – and just enough freedom to bend the rules if required.[8] We explore the importance of this in Habit 8: Balance focus with freedom.

2 Match the right people with the right projects

Take care to recruit the right people to assignments which best fit their capabilities and interests. It is an electric manager's job to make sure that people in the team achieve a good balance of personal challenge, learning and enjoyment from the work. Aardman executive chairman David Sproxton rates the ability to understand the capabilities of your employees, to ensure they are challenged properly, as a 'highly important skill'. It is one of the major transitions of management to realise a good part of your focus now needs to rest with the abilities of others – and not yourself.

3 Manage deadlines carefully

A certain level of urgency is always present in business. It goes with the territory. 'Time is money', as the old cliché goes. And reasonable, genuine deadlines – delivering a proposal, being faster than competitors, meeting client expectations – can help to heighten ingenuity. But research shows there are two types of deadlines that are poison to creativity:[9]

- **Unrealistic deadlines**: constant, overambitious deadlines don't lead to breakthroughs; they lead to nervous breakdowns and talent burnout. Creativity flows from situations where people can explore and play; when they have sufficient time and resources to do the job.

- **'Fake' deadlines**: time limits invented by managers to artificially stimulate people to action don't help; in fact they hinder people's ability to work creatively. Not only are they ineffective, they destroy the relationship between teams and managers because they're (rightly) viewed as manipulative.

If you fail to set realistic, honest deadlines you will encourage the famous response written by English science-fiction novelist Douglas Adams: 'I love deadlines. I like the whooshing sound they make as they fly by.'

4 Protect people in the maze

Imagine a giant maze.[10] The sort of maze with evergreen hedges too high to see over. The maze represents the time a person or team spends trying to apply creativity to a problem. A bad electric manager stands at the edge of the maze with a megaphone shouting: 'Get to the nearest exit; we need to deliver this project right now! And if you do manage to get out in double quick time, you'll be in line for a bonus.' A focus on a specific, speedy outcome backed up by juicy carrots such as cash bonuses encourage people to follow the most well-trodden path. You'll get a result, but it won't be very creative.

If you are trying to escape from a maze very fast they aren't as much fun. In fact they are quite frustrating. But, if you are absorbed in solving the mystery of a maze, they're enjoyable. Time flies. So, the role of a good creative manager is to pat the person or team on the back as they enter the maze – then to stand guard as they roam around inside. The hope is the person or team is motivated to explore the maze, to find interesting pathways and routes inside that are novel and valuable. To encourage this intrinsic, inner desire to crack the code, to unveil the mystery, to be creative, you stand guard at the exit to usher the team back inside if their 'route' is not up to scratch.

A good electric manager will also shield the person or team from the pressures of business life: impatient clients and carping from other parts of the business. Ben Kingsley, who played the lead in the 1982 biopic movie *Gandhi*, tells a story of how the director, Richard Attenborough, skilfully managed his anxiety during a crucial scene. There were hundreds of extras and an enormous crew standing by. The light was fading. Kingsley felt under enormous pressure. But he was struggling to get his lines just right. He recalls how Attenborough paused and whispered in his ear: 'You have all the time in the world, dear boy.' Kingsley nailed the line, Oscars all round.

Creative business managers ensure people and teams have sufficient time and resources to do the job of innovation properly. That means having time to explore, and to think protected from the ever-present need to deliver for customers and clients. John Cleese, the English actor, comedian and management commentator, puts it this way: 'If you want creative workers, give them enough time to play.'

☀ In your next project appoint yourself guardian of the creative maze as your team explore ideas and options.

5 Manage the process

There are many versions of a generic creative process from thinkers going back nearly a hundred years. Here is the version I've designed as a good start for you to tweak and compare with your own team or business.

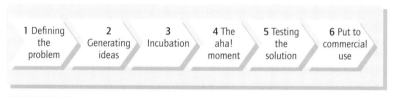

| 1 Defining the problem | 2 Generating ideas | 3 Incubation | 4 The aha! moment | 5 Testing the solution | 6 Put to commercial use |

figure 2.1   The Spark creative process

By all means modify it to match how you work. By understanding the stages you can carefully calibrate your behaviour – what you do and say – to help rather than hinder idea creation. Here are some suggestions for the key milestones in the process – and what can do as a manager to add value.

Creative stage	What's happening	Management action
Defining the problem	Insight and analysis are used to engage with the issue – the search is on for helpful information. This stage is all about ensuring the team has a clear and tight brief to work with.	Ensure the team has a well-written brief and the problem or issue is clearly delineated. Make sure sources of inspiration and information are available so the team start thinking as broadly and creatively as possible.
Generating ideas	Divergent thinking is used to generate lots of different ideas.	Defer judgement until each idea has been fully explored with a 'yes, and...' approach. In reality, groups can self-consciously flip between 'not judging' and 'judging' ideas during this stage, as long as this is facilitated skilfully – that's often the job of the manager – to bring in all the experience and expertise in the room.
Incubation	'Letting go' and allowing the power of the imagination to work in the background.	Hold your nerve! Protect your people from too much interference while this stage runs its course. There may be a slack period when the mysterious workings of the unconscious, 'secret brain' take over. This might look like a waste of money to you (and, more problematically, to your boss or the client); but, clearly it's not. Creativity often strikes when the problem is not front of mind.
The aha! moment	The moment when lightning strikes and a viable idea happens.	Don't get too excited. Business people know this is just the start of turning the idea into something that can help the business or be commercialised. Often the so-called aha! moment is actually a long series of aha! moments, as a mediocre idea is challenged, refined and worked up into something better over weeks, months, or even years.
Testing the idea	Convergent thinking: Does this work to solve our problem or, more subjectively, is this genuinely a 'good idea'?	Listen carefully to your analytical brain and your 'gut'. Does this idea look right, sound right – and feel right? Creative leaders and managers have the courage to stand up for good ideas (and 'good' is always a subjective call) and kill bad ideas (ditto).
Put to commercial use	The idea or solution is implemented in the business.	This is innovation: the role of management is to mobilise coalitions of people to make the idea valuable inside or outside the business.

☀ Consciously choose when to intervene skilfully
and when to step back tactfully during the creative
process. Intervention opportunities include setting
clear goals, keeping the team on track, matching
the right people with the right projects and
supporting the team with time and resources.

Understanding where ideas come from

"All great artists and thinkers are great workers, indefatigable
not only in inventing, but also in rejecting, sifting, transforming,
ordering."
Friedrich Nietzsche, German philosopher

When I mentioned I was writing this book to a friend of mine
who is a senior partner in a British law firm, she said: 'Oh, creativity; we see that as a dark art that nobody properly understands'.
My friend is like so many managers. They know creativity is
important; but it's shunted into the corner, as there isn't the time
or tools to understand it – let alone manage it. Creativity is a black
box that you hope your employees go into every now and then.
You've no idea what happens inside, but you cross your fingers
they'll emerge with a good idea.

If you see creativity as a bit of a grey area, you're in good company.
In the last century, scholars from the fields of psychology, education, philosophy, sociology, linguistics, business management
and economics have disappeared into its mysteries and emerged
with varying, and sometimes conflicting, advice. Even a brief
survey of the ongoing arguments over where ideas emerge from
could fill a dozen pages. I'm going to spare you the detail, and
examine only the key questions for an effective manager within a
creative business:

- How do ideas happen?
- What role does inspiration play?
- What role does good, old-fashioned hard work play?

These are crucial questions for an electric manager – here we'll shed enough light on them to make your job easier.

☀ Think about the last good idea that emerged from your team – how and why did it happen?

The mysteries of a hot shower

Some people argue the very idea of a creative process is like a unicorn or an honest politician: an intriguing concept that doesn't exist in the real world. However, there **is** a creative process and it's very useful for managers to understand it. There is still an ongoing debate over exactly what happens in the creative process and the relative importance of each stage. By briefly illuminating these contradictory viewpoints, I hope to provide you with something solid you can rely on to better manage the process of ideas happening in your business. To simplify things (and believe you me, it needs it) let's weigh both sides of the debate.

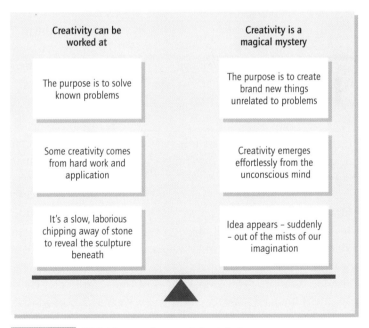

Creativity can be worked at	Creativity is a magical mystery
The purpose is to solve known problems	The purpose is to create brand new things unrelated to problems
Some creativity comes from hard work and application	Creativity emerges effortlessly from the unconscious mind
It's a slow, laborious chipping away of stone to reveal the sculpture beneath	Idea appears – suddenly – out of the mists of our imagination

figure 2.2   Weighing up the creativity debate

Another route to better understand the inherent tension in business creativity is through what psychologists call divergent and convergent thinking models.

- Divergent thinking: here creativity is about widening the scope and **not** judging them, because quantity of ideas will lead to quality of ideas later on.

- Convergent thinking: this involves carefully judging the quality of ideas and using analysis to narrow the scope down to a single 'right answer'.

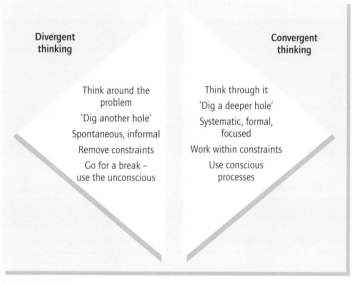

Divergent thinking

Think around the problem
'Dig another hole'
Spontaneous, informal
Remove constraints
Go for a break –
use the unconscious

Convergent thinking

Think through it
'Dig a deeper hole'
Systematic, formal, focused
Work within constraints
Use conscious processes

figure 2.3   Divergent and convergent thinking styles

The secret brain

The most heated arguments are over the role of our unconscious – the 'secret brain' – that works without us knowing. One side of the argument seeks to highlight its role in our personal creativity. Take, for example, 3M's campus HQ in St Paul, Minnesota. There you might imagine red-eyed, industrious workers locked in dark conference rooms sweating over the next big thing. Actually, you would find people engaged in all sorts of frivolous activities from playing pinball to just taking a stroll. Their managers push them to take regular breaks because time away from a problem can help spark a moment of insight. This is because interrupting work with a relaxing activity lets the mind turn inward, where it can puzzle subconsciously over subtle meanings and connections (the brain is incredibly busy when daydreaming). 'That's why so many insights happen during warm showers,' says Joydeep Bhattacharya, a psychologist at Goldsmiths, University of London.

My research and experience points to what most people know intuitively: when you're pondering over something that requires creativity, there is sometimes a mysterious moment when 'something happens'. At the start of my leadership programmes, I always ask participants when and where they benefit from their own personal aha! moments. The answers are, almost always, when the person has switched off from work: out jogging, on their bicycle, driving home and, yes, you guessed it: in the shower. Archimedes may have had his Eureka moment in the bath, but in the modern world many of us are at our most relaxed and subliminally sensitive when we're standing in the shower. It's the one time of the day when our brain can switch off. It's there, and in other unguarded moments, that we can hear our own genius whispering to us.

As a business person, if I could diminish the role of mystery in creativity, I would. Let's face it, the unconscious is the most unreliable employee of all time. It talks to you only in dreams and then in a coded language you don't understand; it has deep urges, some of them, a little antisocial and distinctly sexual; and it reveals its work only when it wants too. The problem is this: I believe these spontaneous 'aha!' moments are the magic and mystery at the heart of a creative business. They have given birth to every patent, new product and successful new company ever known. The challenge for the electric manager is to live with that slightly unnerving knowledge.

Business creativity is not a case of crazy divergent thinking or disciplined, systematic thinking. **It's both**. Both sides of the scales have weight. Creativity is a complex combination of blood, sweat and tears and effortless imagination and dreams. It's a wonderful mystery, and also a (little) explainable. Imagination, the unconscious, whatever you want to call it, **is involved**; but then so are hours of solid, structured application to fully understand the area in which creativity is being used.

Sometimes creativity comes to us in the mists of a hot shower. But, when it doesn't, we have to search it out. After surveying the scientific research into imagination, journalist Jonah Lehrer concluded: 'The reality of the creative process is that it often requires persistence, the ability to stare at a problem until it makes sense. It's forcing oneself to pay close attention, to write all night and then fix those words in the morning. It's sticking with a poem until its perfect; refusing to quit on a maths question; working until the cut of a dress is just right. The answer will be revealed slowly, gradually emerging after great effort.'[11] The classical composer Ludwig Van Beethoven is often cited as almost a cliché of effortless genius. But even the great man struggled with his music and often would make 70 different versions of a musical phrase before it was 'right'.

The creative process needs both cavalier imaginative leaps **and** the remorseless grind of roundhead application and reality. This is why the advertising slang term 'T-Shirts & Suits' to distinguish between 'alien creatives' and 'boring suits' has stuck. The phrase acknowledges that it may not always be the same people bringing these qualities to the party. Deborah Baker, HR director at Sky, puts it this way: 'I believe in balance. You need to have lots of creative people – and lots of people to check their ideas and ensure they work.'

An electric manager certainly has to understand and deploy both approaches. The creative process is messy, paradoxical and difficult to explain because creative people, teams and businesses have to shuttle constantly between divergent and convergent modes of thinking. Creative academic Chris Bilton writes: 'The argument here is not that creative thinkers need to release themselves into a meditative state (the bath), any more than they need to lock themselves into an inexorable process of analysis (the workshop). Instead they need to find a way of changing gears mentally.'[12]

※ Start to better understand your own personal creative process. For example, where and when do you have your 'aha!' moments of insight?

Electric conclusion

To facilitate, support and inspire the creative process, electric managers need to rip up the normal managerial play book and take a distinctly fresh approach. It is tricky because it involves unlearning some of the normal rules of management. At its heart is being constantly aware of when management is useful in the creative process – and when it's not. It requires the sort of self-awareness and bravery normally associated with the leadership attitudes described in the next habit.

Sparks to remember

→ Traditional management doesn't work for business creativity. It kills, rather than encourages, ideas.

→ Electric managers break the rules to find a new, more facilitative style.

→ The managerial approach is grounded in understanding and accepting the inherent paradoxes within the psychology of creativity.

→ Always begin a creative project by defining clear objectives and matching the right people with the right roles.

→ Understand the unique creative process in your business - and then manage it as lightly as possible.

CLEAR steps to change

Communicate

Ask three people to explain your company's creative process – and compare what they tell you. What are the differences – and similarities – in how they map it out?

Learn

Sit down with the key people in your team and draw up:

- your creative process: create a version of what it is now – and 'what it should be';

- your current management interventions: these are the processes and practices you use to monitor activity and drive results: examples include time sheets, six-monthly appraisals, sign-off for investment, how you run your regular management meetings, ad hoc 'check-in' meetings and internal communications.

Energise

Are these management processes and practices empowering people around you to use their initiative, speak up with new ideas and seek to improve the way you work as a business? Or, are they killing creativity? Are your creative process and management interventions good, bad or indifferent? How should they develop? Design a series of sensible changes that will make the biggest difference. Don't implement them all at once. Start small; you can continue the improvement process based on success.

Act

Implement some changes to how you manage your team and business based on the thinking above. Make sure you communicate the reason behind these to those not involved in the initial brainstorming group.

Respond

After six weeks, get the original group back together and ask: What worked? What didn't work? What else needs to change for us to work more creatively?

3

Lead with creative choices
How to choose to be an inspiring leader

You'll learn:

▨ The nine principles of creative leadership, including:
- finding your purpose
- being self-aware and authentic
- pushing for perfection; and
- saying thank you

"A friend, a helper, a guardian, a facilitator, a ... bastard!"
Robert Tammaro, founder and creative director, Undercurrent Brands, when asked to define creative leadership

Sir John Hegarty, the creative co-founder of the legendary advertising agency Bartle Bogle Hegarty (BBH), makes it his business to meet with the 21-year-old graduates joining BBH to explain his leadership philosophy. He tells them:' We are not like other businesses. We are an inverted triangle – and I'm at the bottom. That means you're at the top. The only power I have is to recognise what you have done and push it like crazy. With one great idea you can transform the fortunes of this agency and our client's business. You have that power. The only power I have is the power to commission your work.'

He knows his role is to help lead the company culture: 'You've got to let them know they have permission to fail. There is no such thing as the wrong answer. It's an opinion. There are no facts on the future, as they say. You have got to create a culture where they feel happy. Play is one of the most creative things we do, and people don't play when they're fearful.' He elaborates: 'I don't want anyone second guessing – to be thinking – "what does John want?" I have to let people know I want to buy the ideas they are pitching.'

He is most passionate about how you can support, rather than dictate, direction; especially in the challenging moments when the work he sees is not good enough. He reveals his own method of handing responsibility back to people who pitch ideas to him that don't make the grade. 'I turn to people and say: "This is really good, but is it great?" I want you to be famous. I want you to look back and say: "This was a great moment in my career".' Laughing, he adds: 'Creative people love a challenge!'

He believes in the moment after a first failed attempt a leader can inspire something very special: 'The trick is to find a bit of what they have produced already that is good and focus on that. I need them to walk out feeling – we can crack this! It's vital they don't feel deflated – they must feel passionate, energised and positive. When they leave my room they must feel they can go and do something great. If I belittle them, then I destroy them. Cynicism is the death of creativity. Hitler was very successful for some time. Mussolini made the trains run on time. Arseholes can do great things. But eventually you pay a price for it.'

He even encourages clients to take this attitude too: 'I say to clients: "You've got incredible power. If you make it clear you are here to buy great work, our teams will work three times harder on your brief." The ironic thing is inspiration is free. It can't be bought. I can buy the left side of the brain. I can't buy the right side.'[1]

A beacon of inspiration

A wise man once said: 'Management is doing things right; leadership is doing the right things'.[2] To do the right thing as a creative leader you need to be a beacon of inspiration to those around you. By its nature, creative leadership is the least prescriptive of the habits. That's because it's a deeply personal learning journey that lasts a lifetime. Along the way your development path should be about building your own authentic, inspiring leadership style. But there's no set formula to become a creative leader. They often diverge significantly from what we think of as 'normal leadership'. But, in my work with leaders and managers in countless creative businesses, one thing has become clear: there are identifiable leadership themes and principles that crop up again and again. These are described in this chapter so you can study them, personalise them, and build them into your individual philosophy.

This chapter is about applying creativity to the way you approach your role as a leader. It's a golden opportunity to compare your own principles with those of other leaders. The objective, of course, is to grow your influence within your business. It's about making your leadership challenge a little easier.

Leadership is crucial. Many of us have worked in businesses that have a lot of people in management positions, but a disturbing lack of leaders. And the idea that a creative approach to leadership is important is evidenced by the largest ever study of CEO attitudes. 1,500 corporate and public sector leaders from 60 nations and 33 industries were interviewed. The majority rated creativity as the most important personal quality.[3]

Leadership from every chair

Ideas come from anywhere and everyone. So, creative leadership is not confined to people who sit in the boardroom. The non-hierarchical and meritocratic culture of a creative business means leading is less of an individual pursuit, and more of a team sport, than any other type of organisation. Creativity guru Sir Ken Robinson puts it this way: 'The role of a creative leader is not to have all the ideas; it's to create a culture where everyone can have ideas and feel that they're valued ... it's a big shift for a lot of people.'[4]

Of course, owner-managers, founders and senior executives have to inspire those around them. And middle managers need to lead, too. But this section on creative leadership is not just for people with director, or chief or 'head of' in their title. It's aimed at **everybody** in a creative business. Everybody has to **get** leadership so they can spark electric conversations. Creative businesses encourage leadership from every chair in the office.

Eight principles of creative leadership

Sir John Hegarty's story might make you think creative people make the best creative leaders, but that's not the case. Developing yourself from an expert practitioner into a genuine leader is a challenging transition – and creative people struggle with it. Nick Catliff was a film director before founding the UK production company, Lion TV. He said: 'When you are a practitioner it's all about your vision. When you step up and start employing people, you have to make a big change. Many do it very badly. Their instinct is to tell people what to do. They can't let go; as a result they are very poor leaders. The best creative leaders manage to retain what made them good in the first place – their incisiveness and guts – but allow other people's creativity to flourish.'[5]

Your ability to handle the transition is defined by the creative choices you make: about your own leadership purpose, how you respond to what happens every day, how you stand up for people and ideas – and how you inspire electric conversations. Leadership is highly personal; there is no 'one way' for you to go. But there are eight consistent principles I've seen over and over again, as shown in Figure 3.1.

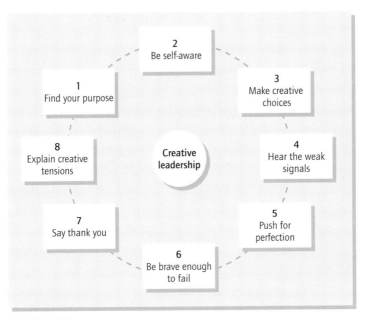

figure 3.1 The eight principles of creative leadership

1 Find your purpose

"If you don't stand for something you will fall for anything."
Malcolm X, American civil rights activist

A creative business relies on its environment – its internal weather system. Leaders play a big part in influencing the weather to be stormy, humid, rainy – or creative. But to change the weather around you, first you have to make your own weather. To pro-actively make your own weather - your emotions, thoughts, attitudes and behaviours - you need to be inspired. But this has a distinct chicken and egg feel to it. To inspire others, first you need to be inspired. And that inspiration comes from inside you. This means leadership is an inside-out development journey. Finding your own inspiring leadership purpose entails committing to a personal journey of self-reflection to discover the sort of leader you **want** to be – with an authentic style that's personal to **you**.

It's about answering the question: 'Why would anyone want to be led by you?'[6]

A big step on that journey is to embrace what you stand for as a business leader. BBH's Sir John Hegarty is very clear about his leadership purpose. It is to: 'Inspire everyone around me.' All of the great creative leaders I've worked with have a clear understanding of their own 'Why?' Don't lead because you got promoted or you have to – because there are no other volunteers. Lead because you want to make an impact on the world.

☀ Explore your 'Why?' Start by making notes on the questions below. Even if the answer is not clear cut, it'll help to define your empowering intention as a creative leader.

- What inspires you?
- Why do you want to lead?
- What do you want to achieve through creative business leadership?

2 Be self-aware

"He who understands others is learned, He who understands himself is wise."
Lao Tse, Chinese philosopher, 6th century BC

You spend most of your time on the 'dance floor' of life. Modern jobs and home life, like a packed, heaving night club, are absorbing places to be. You're encouraged to move in time to music that's often cued up by other people and external events. The alarm clock goes off in the morning like a starting gun, propelling you into frenetic activity. Sometimes, you're dancing alone, wrapped up in a particular issue. At other times, you're fully engaged with those around you. Either way, there's little time or opportunity to observe how well you are dancing, living or leading.

Learning to stand back and see yourself as others see you is crucial to successful creative leadership. It's the ability to step off the dance floor[7]; to walk to the balcony overlooking the throng, and observe your life. To become sufficiently self-aware to stand back and make conscious decisions of how you will respond to what happens to you in any situation. It's the invaluable knack of dispassionately monitoring your own mental, emotional and physical states as you interact with the world around you. Self-awareness is the cornerstone of modern leadership development. It's accepted as crucial for developing an authentic and effective leadership style. It's even more important for creative leaders because so much is expected from them: an ability to engage with people, persuasively communicate ideas, as well as be inspirational to others.

Being authentic

Creative leaders don't need to be perfect, but they do need to be human and real. Finding a clear purpose helps you to be authentic and is a vital part of creative leadership development. You wouldn't think it would be difficult just to be 'authentically you' in a management role, but it is, isn't it? In their study of what makes an authentic leader, London Business School Professors Rob Goffee and Gareth Jones found that inspiring leaders are those that have sufficient self-knowledge to have worked out **what works for them** – and they reveal just enough of themselves to be acknowledged as an authentic leader. In other words, they are themselves, but with more skill.[8] A British TV executive told me about a creative commissioner in the USA who insisted, when teams flew in to pitch their ideas, they sang with him around the piano in his office. Is this authentic and inspiringly risky? Or, is it just a bit embarrassing? You'd have to be in the room to make that call. But creative leaders are not afraid of pushing people out of their comfort zones – and revealing their own unique quirkiness. Revealing yourself involves taking a few risks. But for your colleagues it's living proof that you are a person not just a suit. You need to be able to inspire and motivate people by showing them who you are, what you stand for – and, importantly, what you will and won't do. Goffee and Jones conclude with a warning: 'Showing yourself as a leader always involves risks, and the risks are personal. To imagine you can act as an effective leader without putting a little bit of yourself on the line is an illusion. And a dangerous one.'[9]

☀ Develop enough self-awareness to be able to judge the impact you are having on others. This is an important step on your development path to finding your own authentic leadership style. One route to take: ask some people you trust to list your strengths and weaknesses. Be careful, though, this can freak people out. It's asking for them to be honest with you. Let's face it; we often hide behind politeness, even with our close friends.

3 Make creative choices

"If you can dream - and not make dreams your master; If you can think - and not make thoughts your aim; If you can meet with Triumph and Disaster; And treat those two impostors just the same."
Rudyard Kipling, English poet

Nelson Mandela is judged by many to have been the most inspiring political leader of our time: the only politician in history to be grieved globally. His amazing ability to connect with billions of people was not just down to his perseverance, his improbable Long March to Freedom, or even his one-thousand megawatt charisma. It was driven by the creative choice he made one day in his Robben Island prison cell during his 27 years of incarceration by the South African Government. Instead of reacting in the obvious way - by plotting the downfall of his tormentors - he chose to do the exact opposite. He learned Afrikaans, the language of his jailers, in order to communicate with them. His leadership purpose in life was to make One South Africa, black and white together. His creative choice was to forgive, and even to offer redemption to his white persecutors, in order to live that purpose. There's a reason why Mandela captures the imagination. If he can make such a brave creative choice, can we do the same in our life?

Self-awareness enables creative choices. By examining your thoughts, as they happen, you can influence how you perceive the world. You are able to create your own reality – rather than allowing life to create it for you. It's about using your free will to choose your response to what life throws at you: client wins, client losses; sunshine and rain, sickness and health. The key to truly transformative creative choices is to defer judgement: to refuse to label life's external events as 'good' or 'bad'. Instead think: 'How can I respond creatively to this situation to get the best result?' By leading yourself more consciously, you're able to more effectively lead and inspire others.

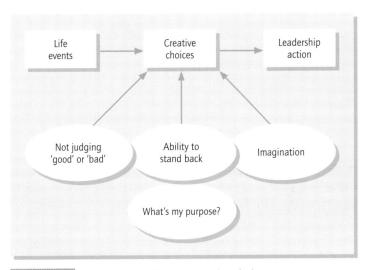

figure 3.2   **Making space for your creative choices**[10]

☀ Leaders inspire because of the conscious creative choices they make in response to life events. Next time something big happens, don't choose your first knee-jerk response. Pause to make a creative choice. Then act decisively. Maybe there is a different attitude you could take to a tough situation you're facing right now? Be imaginative.

As long as you can accept your new attitude, or response, it's valid.

4 Hear the faint signals

"The simple act of paying positive attention to people has a great deal to do with productivity."
Tom Peters, management guru

Creative leaders spend less time telling, and more time truly communicating: **listening** as well as speaking. I've been lucky enough to work with Dame Gail Rebuck, the chairman of Penguin Random House's British operations. I interviewed her in the months after the merger between Random House and Penguin, which created the biggest book publisher in the world. She maintained that one of the most useful things any leader can learn is to listen very carefully for new ideas, problems or opportunities. She describes an ability to detect things that are vitally important, but are not obvious unless you are 'in the moment' with your sixth sense switched on. 'Creative leadership is about listening for the faint signals inside and outside the business. It's another way of using your instincts,' she said. 'You'll never be on top of all the detail in a company. But you could be in an elevator listening to a particular conversation, or have a chance meeting as you buy your sandwich. Someone says something which illuminates some aspect of the business. And you think: "'Oh, that's interesting" or "That's a problem," and respond. It's about being a listening organisation.'

This ability to listen and observe with real intensity – what a colleague of mine[11] calls 'X-Ray listening'– is connected to the open style that leaders need to use in a creative business. As someone who works with organisations and leaders – sometimes as a coach – I see the obvious connections between empowering creative leadership and the techniques that underpin coaching itself. Coaching is about using the power of open questions that provoke a full response rather than a straight 'yes' or 'no'. For example, 'Why?' is always an open question.

Creative leaders need to use questions and active listening to help people to find their own best solution to a problem. The objective of any interaction is not to tell them what to do but to raise people's awareness of the issues at hand and sharpen their feelings of responsibility to get it done. Good teachers tell people where to look; not what to see. You start with the belief that people are fundamentally good enough to do the job; they have untapped potential and, if empowered, will find their own solutions.[12] Developing a listening sixth sense is about becoming a skilled observer of people and their motivations. When I met with Stuart Murphy, Sky's Director of Entertainment Channels, he reflected: 'One of the things you need in a creative business is to read rooms and understand people. I almost think there should be an obligatory psychology exam for managers and bosses. My job is to make sure I see where people can fly. What buttons to push for each particular person.'[13]

☀ Listen to the faint signals. Hidden in the whispers and white noise is where your leadership focus should be – or the next big idea for your business.

5 Push for perfection

Steve Jobs worked and innovated in a number of industries. So, as well as co-founding the computer business Apple, he also co-founded Pixar Animation. During the development of almost every product he ever created, Jobs at some point 'hit the pause button' and went back to the drawing board because he felt it failed to be perfect. Take the Pixar animated movie, *Toy Story*. After Disney chairman Jeffrey Katzenberg bought the rights to the film, he pushed the Pixar team to make it edgier and darker. Jobs and the visionary director John Lasseter resisted. The impasse became so great, the pair finally halted production to completely rewrite the script to make it even more friendly and warm. This was highly unusual, expensive and risky. Of course, they were right, and the rest is cinematic history. *Toy Story* went on to earn hundreds of millions of dollars worldwide. It's widely considered by many critics to be one of the best animated films ever made.

At Apple, Jobs also hit the pause button on the iPhone. The initial design had the glass screen set into an aluminium case. Jobs went to over to see the head designer Jonathon Ive. 'I didn't sleep last night because I realised that I just didn't love it,' he said. Ive saw, to his dismay, that Jobs was right. 'I remember feeling absolutely embarrassed that he had to make the observation.' Jobs helped Ive to see the whole device felt too masculine, task-driven and efficient. After nine months of hard work, the team tore up their designs and started again. 'It was one of my proudest moments at Apple,' Jobs said.

A creative leader needs to push for perfection. This theme is picked up in the advertising agency Ogilvy & Mather's staff manual. It urges everyone in the agency to become an uncompromising perfectionist: 'Don't bow your head. Don't know your place. Defy the gods. Don't sit back. Don't give in. Don't give up. Don't win silvers. Don't be so easily happy with yourself. Don't be spineless. Don't be gutless. Don't be toadies. Don't be Gollum. Don't go gently into that good night. And don't **ever, ever** allow a single scrap of rubbish out of the agency.'

It's about an obsession with quality. Pixar's John Lasseter said: 'Quality is the best business plan of all.'[14] The same tough streak can be seen in how creative leaders connect with employees. They are the first in line to elevate and protect talented people. But, because creative quality and ideas are so important, they are not afraid to review the effectiveness of people on an ongoing basis. Paul Kitcatt, founder of the London-based digital agency Kitcatt Nohr Digitas, is a softly spoken and thoughtful man. He's known as a humane, empathetic and supportive leader. But, when I met him in London, he admitted to me: 'I'm not going to pretend creatives go on being wonderful forever, even in our regime. Clearly they don't. People lose direction and motivation and what you then have to do is talk to them about it ... people do lose their jobs. That does happen.'[15]

☀ Protect ideas while they're small green shoots, and the people who need some time. But it cuts both ways. Sometimes you need to be a 'bastard'. You must kill bad ideas and refresh the team when required. Is there an idea being developed that

doesn't make the grade? Is there a person that
needs to refocus on another project – or perhaps be
shown towards the door marked 'exit'?

6 Be brave enough to fail

"If we knew what we were doing it wouldn't be research."
Albert Einstein

A Formula 1 motor racing journalist once asked the legendary
risk-taking and creative F1 driver, James Hunt: 'James, what's the
secret to winning?' Hunt paused for effect, and then deadpanned
back to the startled reporter: 'Big balls'. The creative process is
painful, messy and risky. Like Hunt, it doesn't race along in nice
neat lines; it's unpredictable and, during the development and
launch phases, you won't know how things will work out. You
need to have 'big balls' to stake your reputation and hard-earned
money on what often will amount to hunches.

The Hollywood screenwriter William Goldman, who wrote the
scripts for films such as *Butch Cassidy and the Sundance Kid* and *All
the President's Men*, argues that nobody knows which films will
be successful and which ones will sink without trace. Even with
audience focus groups, this is still true today. It is why Hollywood
seems to retreat to turgid summer blockbusters supported by massive marketing machines or incessant sequels. These are more
likely to offer a guaranteed return on investment, so they require
significantly less bravery to 'green light'.

☀ Prepare for failure. When times are good,
creative leaders store up a 'winners' reputation like
squirrels do with their food in summer. From time
to time a project will fail and winter will come and
dent your reputation. Accept it.

Part of the challenge of creative leadership is living with risk. If
the leader of a creative business doesn't show bravery and stand
up for new ideas, who will? A tongue-in-cheek Ogilvy & Mather
anecdote amusingly illustrates what happens when teams
become timid and seek to lower the risk of a new advertising campaign to zero:

"The creative director thought it was funny. The managing director thought it was funny.

The chairman thought it was funny. The tea lady thought it was funny.

The client thought it was funny. The client's wife thought it was funny. The client's butcher thought it was funny.

Okay now, let's research it to see if it's funny."[16]

A creative leader needs to encourage people to be brave enough to take risks, and safe enough to fail. 'Part of our culture is that we celebrate failure,' says John Herlihy, who heads up Google's European operations centre in Ireland. 'It's okay to fail here. If you are not failing enough, then you are not taking enough risks. When the Romans used to ransack Europe, they had this fantastic model where they would send scouts out in five different directions. The four that didn't come back, they knew not to go in that direction. So what we do here is fail, and fail fast.'[17]

Sir Richard Branson, founder of the Virgin empire, points out the value in failure: 'You don't learn to walk by following rules. You learn by doing, and by falling over.' So, a skilled creative leader must accept failure and point out how it can be useful learning. Of course, you must not flinch from assessing why things have gone wrong and ensuring it doesn't happen again. But, where required, you must vigorously protect the people behind the failed new app, cleaning product, recruitment service or CRM system. The same mistakes should never be made twice; but failure is part of the creative business model – and the buck stops with you.

So – if failure is such a big part of successful innovation – why are businesses so risk averse? Wally Olins is one of the world's leading practitioners in branding and identity, and was chairman of the company which came up with the mobile phone brand, Orange. 'Why is it the case that large, global companies tend not to innovate?' he asks, 'Why are they frightened of creative solutions? Because they have a defensive mentality, because they listen too much to what focus groups tell them. They tend not to trust their own judgement or the expertise of their creative advisors. That's why, when they have failed to innovate, they have to go out and buy a small company that can and does.'[18]

A senior luxury goods executive from the handbags, fashion, perfume and champagne giant LVMH once demonstrated to me what commercial bravery should feel like. I asked him how much research he did to get the right materials, tailoring, look and feel for next year's line. He turned to me and declared with a heavy French accent: 'We don't ask people what they want next; we tell them.'

To get over their quite sensible fear, leaders need to fight against their own pre-programmed human nature. Human beings are hardwired to dismiss challenging new ideas on first contact. Studies show, independent of other factors, the more often people are exposed to something, the more positive they feel about it. But when things are brand new, rare and unfamiliar they will often provoke negative reactions. Stanford University psychologist Robert Zajonc calls this the 'mere exposure effect'. This human predisposition to think new-is-bad, familiar-is-good has been found with things as diverse as shapes, photographs of faces, random sequences of tone, food, odours, flavours, colours and people. We're mostly unaware of the effect and routinely deny it happens; but it does.

☀ New ideas scare people. The best way to mitigate this fact of human nature is to become a world-class, confident pitcher of ideas. And to learn to trust your own instincts.

Bravery sometimes means introducing a little chaos: after all, creative tension starts from the top. Some have taken it upon themselves to become the Trouble-Maker-in-Chief in their own business. Founder of Ogilvy & Mather, David Ogilvy, wrote: 'We have a habit of divine discontent with our performance. It is an antidote to smugness.'[19] The current generation of Ogilvy leaders recall: 'David never **entirely** grew up. He would heckle in meetings, throw chocolate cakes at dinner parties and roll down grassy slopes in Brooks Brothers suits.'[20]

☀ **Don't discourage awkward questions. Lead the discordant, disruptive volley of discomforting queries about the status quo.**

The media streaming company Netflix tells its staff they must be careful not to cause an irrevocable financial disaster or a catastrophic legal issue but, that aside: 'Rapid recovery is the right model. Just fix problems quickly. We're in a creative-inventive market, not a safety critical market like medicine or nuclear power. You may have heard preventing error is cheaper than fixing it. Yes, in manufacturing or medicine. Not so in creative environments.'[21]

Saatchi & Saatchi's million-dollar cheque

Advertising agency Saatchi & Saatchi is now one of the world's leading creative organisations with over 4,500 people and 130 offices in 70 countries – and part of Publicis Groupe, the world's third-largest communications group. The agency works with 6 of the top 10, and over half of the top 50, global advertisers. But in 1997 things were very different. 'At the time, the business was on the brink of disaster,' Saatchi & Saatchi's deputy chairman Richard Hytner told me over Earl Grey tea at their UK headquarters in Charlotte Street, London. 'The founders Maurice and Charles had quit. They had gone to set up their own business. The company they left was bleeding cash, losing clients, losing people.'[22]

Turnaround Chairman Bob Seelert rolled the dice and hired the maverick British marketeer Kevin Roberts to change the fortunes of the business. One of Roberts's first acts as worldwide CEO was to write a highly symbolic cheque from Saatchi & Saatchi's dwindling investment fund for $1 million. The recipient of the cheque was Bob Isherwood, the worldwide creative director. He was briefed to spend it as he saw fit to put Saatchi & Saatchi back on the map as a creative force. Hytner said the message to staff and clients must have been clear. The cheque made a statement: 'This company has the unreasonable power of creativity at its heart.' The prime directive for a creative leader is to be brave enough to champion talented people and good ideas. Or sometimes, as Kevin Roberts did, to stand up for the importance of creativity itself.

☀ As a creative leader you'll need to take risks to stand up for good ideas and talented people – and, occasionally, go to bat for creativity itself.

7 Say thank you

"Respect is how to treat everyone, not just those you want to impress."
Sir Richard Branson, founder of Virgin

However outwardly confident and decisive they are, creative leaders often display a curious humility. A lot is made of the value of charisma. But creative leaders tend to be humble about their own contributions; charismatic in a different way. This stems from the realisation, however creative they are personally, they are not the sole fount of ideas – even if they were when the business began its life. They allow ideas to bubble up from the bottom, in fact they encourage it.

Lion TV managing director Nick Catliff recognises the tension between humility and ego: 'When you're the leader you cannot be too dominant – you can't be the "biggest dog in the room" anymore. It's a tension between steering and pushing an idea forward, making it happen, but listening to others. But you also need to be very confident in your judgement. As the leader it will probably be you who pitches the idea to clients, or the boss. And pitching is all about walking into a room and believing in yourself and the idea. In our industry 99 per cent of pitches end in failure. For that you need a pretty robust ego.'[23] Robust ego with tough personality always needs to be balanced with humility. Ben Zander, conductor of the Boston Philharmonic Orchestra, once shared with me his simple but compelling insight: a conductor doesn't play a note, but leads the orchestra to play perfectly in tune and on tempo to make beautiful music.[24]

An acknowledgement of the value of others isn't just about generosity; it's based on a sensible survival instinct. Researchers analysed an internet start-up offering a new, sophisticated form of computer graphics from its inception to its collapse seven years later. While the business enjoyed initial success, ultimately it was unsustainable because it depended too much on the genius of its award-winning founder and took organisational creativity for granted.[25]

☀ Share the responsibility for the generation and development of new ideas, or you will fail as a leader.

I've witnessed 'I-can-do-it-all-syndrome' many times. Diego Rodriguez, a partner at the award-winning global design firm IDEO, calls this the 'lone inventor myth'. He argues that in modern business most innovations draw on many contributions.[26] When I worked with a renowned senior TV executive, developing her leadership team, she made a point of travelling around the global businesses to listen and to hear how ideas had made it on the screen in regular informal get-togethers. It was her way of learning and acknowledging creative people working on the best programmes.

The scarcest resource in any business is time; but creative leaders need to be able to find enough of it to say thank you, to acknowledge great work. In several decades of studying business creativity, US academic Teresa Amabile highlights simple encouragement as a vital success factor. She writes that good managers 'freely and generously recognise creative work by individuals and teams often before the ultimate commercial impact of those efforts is known.' By contrast, bad managers kill creativity 'by failing to acknowledge innovative efforts or by greeting them with scepticism'.

☀ Never forget: a simple thank you goes a very long way. But balance humility with sufficient self-regard to have the guts to pitch a new idea confidently to any audience.

8 Explain creative tensions

Leaders need to be comfortable with the Yin and Yang of creative business. Creative businesses – and the people who lead them – are like circus performers who teeter on rolling steel drums with a foot planted at opposite ends of a plank balanced on the top. They need to make the constant adjustments necessary to hold the equilibrium. It isn't a simple black or white response to the question: 'Are we creative or commercial … are we A or B?' The answer must be: 'We are both creative and commercial – we're A **and** B.'

The tension at the heart of a creative business is the constant discussion, debate and occasional battle between creativity and making a profit. The creative versus commercial tug-of-war needs to go on forever. An honourable tie is what we're looking for; but with creativity celebrated more obviously, widely and passionately. Jeremy Shaw, the chief operating officer of digital advertising agency Kitcatt Nohr Digitas, concluded there is something to be gained by letting all staff know how they have spent their days and weeks on timesheet records to make the link between activity and profitability. But he doesn't run this exercise on a weekly, or even monthly, basis; he knows this would emphasise profit too much.

Steve Jobs was aware of this balance at the heart of creative business. At the end of his famous product demonstrations, Jobs finished by showing a sign at the intersection of 'Liberal Arts and Technology Streets'.[27] He knew creativity occurs when different attitudes, knowledge sets and disciplines intersect. He was a leader that connected creativity to technology; art to engineering. There were always better techies (Bill Gates for one) and better designers (Jobs hired one: Jonathan Ive). But Jobs was a connector that allowed electricity to flow between the two opposite poles. A creative leader must embrace opposites and demonstrate that they're **not** mutually exclusive. In this way you can transform normal business wisdom into creative business wisdom. Creative businesses must embrace the fact opposites can – and do – live together under one roof.[28] After all, the clue is in the seemingly odd bedfellows of the two-word descriptor:

creative + business.

Sometimes it's not about balancing opposing ideas – but about resolving tension by transforming people's views of what a business is all about. A creative leader becomes an expert in translating that language of normal business into creative business speak (see Figure 3.3).

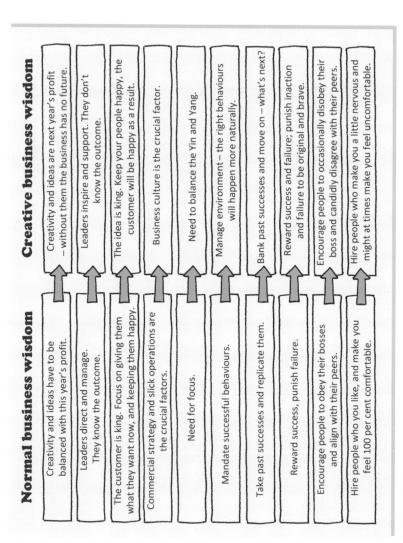

Normal business wisdom

Creativity and ideas have to be balanced with this year's profit.

Leaders direct and manage. They know the outcome.

The customer is king. Focus on giving them what they want now, and keeping them happy.

Commercial strategy and slick operations are the crucial factors.

Need for focus.

Mandate successful behaviours.

Take past successes and replicate them.

Reward success, punish failure.

Encourage people to obey their bosses and align with their peers.

Hire people who you like, and make you feel 100 per cent comfortable.

Creative business wisdom

Creativity and ideas are next year's profit – without them the business has no future.

Leaders inspire and support. They don't know the outcome.

The idea is king. Keep your people happy, the customer will be happy as a result.

Business culture is the crucial factor.

Need to balance the Yin and Yang.

Manage environment – the right behaviours will happen more naturally.

Bank past successes and move on – what's next?

Reward success and failure; punish inaction and failure to be original and brave.

Encourage people to occasionally disobey their boss and candidly disagree with their peers.

Hire people who make you a little nervous and might at times make you feel uncomfortable.

figure 3.3   Translating normal business into creative business speak

☀ Explain the inherent tensions in a creative organisation – and clearly point out the gap between normal and creative business.

Electric conclusion

Creative leadership is a lifelong journey. It is about finding the spark inside you that will help kindle a spark in others. There is no formula, but you can speed up your personal development by understanding and practising the eight key principles in this habit – and combining these with your own unique approach and style.

Sparks to remember

➤ Your leadership will be defined by the proactive, conscious creative choices you make.

➤ To inspire others; first you need to be inspired.

➤ Learning to stand back and see yourself is crucial to your leadership development.

CLEAR steps to change

Communicate

Get some honest feedback from trusted colleagues on your strengths, weaknesses and style as a leader.

Learn

Sit down and ask yourself the question: Why would anyone want to be led by me?

Another structured and powerful way to develop self-awareness is to study any 360-degree feedback information or psychometric tests that your company might arrange. Sometimes your HR department will provide someone to formally debrief you on these.

Finally, participate in any executive coaching or leadership development programme on offer. If your business says there's no budget – make sure to be disciplined about using the exercises in this book – they're free!

Energise

Write a list of your current leadership strengths and weaknesses based on your feedback. Next to each one put a specific action you intend to take to build on this strength or address the weakness.

Sit down with a blank sheet of paper. Think honestly about the non-negotiable principles – your personal values – that ideally you would like to embody at work. Be creative – if you like lists, do that. If you want to write something longer – a manifesto – do that. Don't expect to have the answer first time around – the thinking process is more important than the initial answers. When you have a list of more than three, think about what you could do to better live these values as a leader. Put another way, how could the way you lead – your day-to-day behaviour – better reflect what you believe in? What do you need to do more of? What do you need to do less of? What do you need to start? What do you need to stop? From this long list narrow down to your leadership purpose: a shorter phrase you can bring to mind when you need some guidance.

Act

Change your behaviour for a month, based on the leadership resolutions you made. Go back to your trusted colleagues to find out if they noticed a positive difference. Think about the results you achieved in this month. A good way to keep track is to keep a leadership journal for this period.

Respond

Focus on your successes. What worked for you? How much closer are you to developing your own personal style of leadership? Repeat this exercise in three months. Leadership is a lifelong journey.

4

Become a talent impresario
How to fill your business with creative talent

You'll learn:

- How to hire the right people
- How to manage for inner motivation
- How to encourage 24/7 learning and development
- How to retain the brightest sparks
- How to run your business like a world-class sports team

"It's about getting the best people, retaining them, nurturing a creative environment and helping to find a way to innovate."[1]
Marissa Mayer, CEO of Yahoo!

In 1991 Philip Chin and his wife Joanna founded Langland in their dining room with no money, a printer and a borrowed Apple Macintosh computer. They based the business away from the bright lights of London in sleepy Windsor, in Berkshire. It's fair to say that Windsor isn't a renowned creative hotspot; it's more famous for being home to a royal castle and Legoland. Despite this handicap, by 2007, the couple had built the agency to a very respectable size.

Langland specialises in advertising campaigns on behalf of pharmaceutical companies to promote prescription medicines to healthcare professionals. Healthcare advertising is a niche category which, to put it politely, is viewed by the rest of the advertising industry as a little backward. 'Back in 2007, it was grim. The standard of creative work in the industry was pretty rubbish,' said Chin. Laughing, he added: 'The talent pool is a bit "in-bred", and the quality of creative work lags well behind that seen in consumer advertising. To make a career, you don't generally come to work in healthcare; you're sent.' [2]

But, amid the uninspiring ads for angina tablets, thrush cream and flu jabs, the couple sensed an opportunity. After all, why did they have to conform to low standards? Why not use creativity to transform their business – and the image of the healthcare advertising sector? The tenure of a talented interim creative director, Gordon Torr, provided the perfect opportunity to drive change. Because Langland had been well run they knew they had the cash reserves to invest. Chin said: 'For people to be creative, a business has to be secure. People can't be worried where the next client, or pay cheque, is coming from.' They had also built a solid team, with an empowering culture based on shared values. But they knew there was a missing ingredient. They needed what Chin describes as a 'creative catalyst'. They upped the salary budget so they could bring in someone working from 'outside the healthcare village', and went looking. They found Andrew Spurgeon who had previously been appointed as the youngest creative director in the global JWT advertising agency network.

Chin reflected: 'We had all the ingredients already. We had people with talent, but it was sort of dormant. Andrew came in and worked to bring the talent out. He improved the ones that were average – to good; and those that were good – to great.' More discipline was introduced into the creative process. Three creative principles – simplicity, surprise and empathy – were created and used to judge every piece of creative work. 'Creativity is so subjective,' Chin argues, 'You need to be able to agree a benchmark. At the same time we also improved our standards of production. It's all very well having good ideas; but you also need to execute them brilliantly, with craft skills of the highest order.'[3]

The results of this creative inflection point have been spectacular. In four years Langland transformed itself into 'the world's most creatively awarded healthcare advertising agency'. In 2008, the business won just 24 awards; 4 years later, they won 103. 'It became a bit embarrassing,' Chin ruefully admitted. 'One awards night we were up against the Big Five global advertising agency networks and we walked away with over half of the awards.' At the same time, Langland was recognised as a great place to work and this award was repeated two years in a row.

Leveraging the value of its existing talent through a catalysing new hire has meant that commercial success has accompanied creative excellence. Whilst the rest of its industry shrank, or kicked its heels through the worst downturn in living memory, Langland grew revenues by 45 per cent. Inspired by their purpose statement – 'To be famously creative, effective and profitable' – Chin and Joanna are now focused on expansion. But they're sticking to the formula that's worked so well. Chin concluded: 'It's about talent. Creative businesses are people businesses. It's about relationships. We are now focused on developing our talent to take us forward.'

Has your rocket got the right fuel?

Without the right talent on board, a creative business is like a rocket without fuel. Leaders need to be able to find people with ability, encourage them, develop them, and offer them an environment in which they can flourish. It's the difference between success and failure. One thing's for sure: if you don't understand how people tick, you can't understand how creative business works. Like a TV talent show judge, creative leaders need to be passionate and informed about discovering new talent – and decisive with those that don't make the grade.

☀ Normal businesses can afford to be customer-
focused. Creative businesses have a triple focus: the
idea, the customer and the talent.

A-list talent: small differences, big money

After studying commercial creativity in a wide variety of settings
– the visual and performing arts, films, theatre, sound record-
ings, and book publishing – Harvard Professor Richard Caves
came to a solid conclusion: talent drives success. As a renowned
economist, Caves bought a distinctly analytical, scientific
approach to identifying value drivers within creative businesses.
He argues that even small differences in talent will lead to huge
differences in financial success. He calls this economic rule the
A-list/B-list factor.[4] For example, a movie script placed in the
hands of an A-list film director like Steven Spielberg, the master
storyteller behind *E.T.*, *Jaws* and *Saving Private Ryan*, would produce Movie A. If the same script is directed by a B-list director
with a little less talent, we could compare Movie B to Spielberg's
Movie A. Even though the B-list director might be just as experienced, the finished product will not be separated by a few small
steps. Movies A and B will be a huge leap apart in class. This is
why Hollywood stars like Tom Cruise, and global sports talent
like Cristiano Ronaldo, command fees measured in tens of millions of pounds. Meanwhile, actors and ordinary footballers,
who are still way more talented than 99.9 per cent of the planet,
struggle by on minimum fees and waiting tables. Small differences add up to huge chasms in value. The agents and managers
of Cruise and Ronaldo see the difference between A-list and B-list
talent. In the same exponential way talent impacts the fortunes
of any creative business.

The bozo explosion

Apple's late CEO Steve Jobs was well aware of the crucial role
played by talented people. Biographer Walter Isaacson observed

that Jobs tolerated only what he called A players. Isaacson wrote: 'Jobs was famously impatient, petulant, and tough with people around him. But his treatment of people, though not laudable, emanated from his passion for perfection and his desire to work with only the best. It was his way of preventing what he called "the bozo explosion" in which managers are so polite that mediocre people feel comfortable sticking around.'[5]

I wouldn't advise any leader to use Steve Jobs' managerial approach as a template. Copying a leadership myth is a dangerous game. He was undoubtedly successful; but he was also a complex, idiosyncratic, contradictory character. Working out which factors of his leadership style were positive and negative is difficult. His leadership abilities may have been overestimated – Apple may well have achieved stellar success despite some of his questionable tactics. We'll never know for certain. One thing's for sure: he somehow managed to engender loyalty in his top people; they tended to stick around longer than executives at rival companies with a better reputation for being nice.[6] Clearly he understood the need for hiring the best people: the likes of John Lasseter, Jonathan Ive and Steve Wozniak. And, his preoccupation with talent is a legitimate creative business habit you can seek to emulate.

It's obvious that talent equals creative success. The how is less obvious; that's what this chapter is about. An old-fashioned word for someone who brings people together to put on a theatre production is an impresario. This habit highlights five steps to take to become a talent impresario: to have an obsession with hiring, developing and retaining the best people.

The five steps of the talent impresario habit follow the talent journey from outside your business to making an impact inside it. If enacted consistently, they create a virtuous circle to help you win the war for talent.

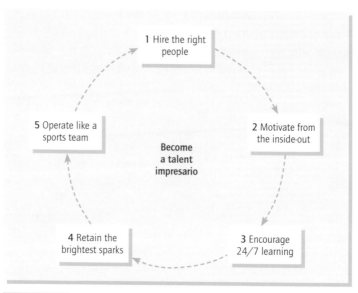

figure 4.1   Five steps to becoming a talent impresario

1 Hire the right people

"Beware of sad dogs that spread gloom."
David Ogilvy, founder of Ogilvy & Mather

Hiring the right people is a critical discipline for a creative business to get right. Jim Collins, the author of *Good to Great*, the iconic business book about lasting success, puts it this way: 'You absolutely must have the discipline **not to hire** until you find the right people.' Former global creative director for the advertising agency JWT, Gordon Torr, who I mentioned previously when he worked with Langland, has written a book about managing creative people. He offers a simple maxim: 'Hire the best talent and let them get on with it.' It's not quite that simple – but his view highlights the importance of talent on the front line. Here is another passionate plea from the global advertising agency Ogilvy & Mather's *Guide to Recruiting Talent*:

> **"There isn't a single activity in our business more important than recruitment. It determines whether or not the**

agency will remain healthy. Every act of recruitment that brings in someone better – better than before or better than average – makes it more likely that we will be successful. Each time we bring in someone who is not good enough, it makes it more likely that we will fail. And it works like a disease with a multiplying effect – because a below-average individual will always, in turn, bring in others who are below average. And so on! Until, in a matter of a few short years, the agency turns from energetic to flat and from vibrant to sad."

How to spot creative people at interview

All people have the capacity to be more creative. But, like sprinting, solving crossword puzzles or cooking a soufflé, some people will be born with more aptitude than others. So, while creativity lurks inside all of us, it makes sense to hire people who've got more than their fair share in the first place. Hiring the right people is a lot cheaper than trying to mould them into the right stuff after they have ripped open their induction pack. Here are a few traits you should be looking for in a person's CV, testimonials and at the interview stage:

- **Their relationship to financial reward is more complex:** The Harvard economist Richard Caves calls this propensity to be more interested in the work than the money: 'art for art's sake'. It has been shown in numerous studies that money does not necessarily buy more creativity. Creative people will be fascinated by how they can develop their own skills, the quality of the clients and projects they have the opportunity to work with. They will be less interested in salary and rewards than people with less creative drive. But don't take this to mean they come cheap. They know their worth and will expect market rates just like anyone else.

- **They define their identity as creative, rather than corporate:** Research shows that for creative people their talent is central to their identity. They are defined by their passion and perfectionism. They may rank their creative identity above being a member of your team. Their loyalty is to their own development and the work – not to you. One way to help them sign up and stay with your business is to ensure they can connect to other clever, creative people inside and outside your organisation. Sell this as a benefit.

- **They are not impressed by corporate hierarchy**: They know their worth in the talent marketplace, and often are organisationally savvy. They relentlessly interrogate team leaders with difficult questions. Once on board they will expect instant access. In response to this tendency Sir Martin Sorrell, founder of the global advertising agency network, WPP, has developed a notable speed of response to emails from his thousands of staff – normally within hours.

- **They will challenge you**: Stanford University management and engineering professor Robert Sutton studied creative businesses and concluded that managers should be searching for a quality that makes them feel just a little bit uncomfortable. He urges managers to hire what he describes as 'low self-monitors'. He writes: 'People who are especially insensitive to subtle, and even not so subtle, hints from others about how to act. For better or worse, low self-monitors are relatively unfettered by social norms. These mavericks and misfits can drive bosses and co-workers crazy, but they increase the range of what is thought, noticed, said, and done in a company.' So you need to assess if the person has talent, of course – but also a certain attitude and a little determined ignorance of 'the right way to do things'. Our natural urge is to hire people like us; but they also need to have the strength of character to challenge the status quo to support a good idea. There is more to a creative business than building a be-like-me cult.

Ask interviewees to explain the ideas and innovations for which they have been responsible in their previous jobs or university career. If they don't respond with passion and enthusiasm, and some compelling examples, they haven't developed

a creative attitude and track record. Also, engineer
a chance for them to candidly disagree with your
opinion to check how independent-minded they are.

Making waves

Hiring is so important because of the greater responsibility placed
on new entrants in a creative environment. Normal businesses
interview candidates with an emphasis on fitting the right person
to the right job. Creative businesses are hoping new people will
bring in new ideas, attitudes and ways of doing things. A senior
executive in a toy company tells of the challenge of hiring people
who 'think like us' – but also retain the ability to point out what's
wrong with existing products. She said the behaviour of new creative employees 'makes us hate them'; but ruefully admitted their
criticism is vital as it leads to new toy ideas.

It took 15 years of frustration, perseverance, and over 5,000
prototypes for the British inventor James Dyson to launch the
first vacuum cleaner under his own name. Within 22 months
it became the best-selling vacuum cleaner in the UK. The company now designs and manufactures hand dryers, bladeless fans
and heaters – selling machines in over 50 countries and employing 3,000 people worldwide – with revenues of over £1.2 billion
and profit margins near 20 per cent.[7] Dyson has prided himself
on delivering products that work in different and better ways.
The same goes for the management of the business. He believes
one reason his company invents successful products is that it
employs a high proportion of graduates straight from university.
He comments: 'They are unsullied. They have not been strapped
into a suit and taught to think by a company with nothing on
its mind but short-term profit and early retirement.'[8] He adds:
'Sometimes breaking convention creates a better way...it's these
bright young minds that offer a glimmer of the engineering stars
of the future.'[9]

☀ Don't hire people because you think they'll swim
with the tide. Hire them because they'll create waves.

Yin and Yang of hiring

Like every other factor in creative business, hiring involves managerial paradox; you having to balance the yin and the yang to get the right result. On the one hand you want to hire people who are creative mavericks who might make waves from time to time. On the other you want them to buy into your company values and purpose – and be able to display sufficient people skills to collaborate successfully with others.

I once visited the UK headquarters of the US games developer and publisher Electronic Arts (EA) to meet with executive vice-president David Gardner. Gardner joined what was a fledgling West Coast company as a teenager in 1983. He was entrusted with setting up their European operations in London just four years later. He spoke affectionately of the stringent recruitment policies the business had in its early years in California. New people coming into EA in the early 1980s didn't meet just one or two people – they were interviewed by everyone in the company. Gardner explained this was deemed necessary to find the 'right kind of people' who fitted EA's creative culture.

☀ Balance the Yin and Yang of hiring.

- **Yin**: Find people who will challenge the status quo.
- **Yang**: Hire them if they'll sign up to your values.

You need a little chemistry with colleagues. History is littered with creative scientists, producers, designers, sportsmen and others who have flourished within one organisation and quietly died in another because of a lack of fit. London Business School Professor Lynda Gratton researched the factors that produce cooperative teams and found parts of the hiring process were crucial.[10] She recommends managers should:

- check if people are cooperative when you hire them;
- design the induction process so cooperation and relationship-building are seen to be important;
- encourage peer-to-peer working – emphasise no one can do it on their own and create easy structures and processes to make it possible.

☀ Ask candidates how they've collaborated in
the past. Listen carefully for how they describe the
contribution of their colleagues. If it's all about
them, thank them politely and show them the door.

2 Motivate from the inside-out

"The happiest thought of my life."
Albert Einstein (referring to the moment when he 'discovered' relativity)

How do you motivate someone to be creative? It is a central
question for a business aspiring to deliver innovation. Harvard
Business School's Teresa Amabile is one of the world's most
respected authorities on business creativity. Bringing together
decades of rigorous psychological, sociological and business field-
work, her words should act as a stark warning: 'There can be no
doubt: creativity gets killed much more often than it gets supported.' For the most part, this isn't because managers have a
vendetta against creativity. They understand the value of ideas.
Creativity is always undermined unintentionally: usually in the
pursuit of 'no-brainer' business goals such as coordination, productivity and control.

To avoid killing creativity, leaders need to understand the three
crucial elements that Amabile's research consistently finds high-
performing creative businesses encourage in their people:

- **Skill**: Founded on technical, procedural; and intellectual
  expertise. Being good at a certain skill - achieving mastery in
  it - is the minimum requirement for commercial creativity.
  This is your craft: from editing video to mining iron ore,
  designing mobile phones to providing legal advice, farming
  pigs to running health clubs. And, of course, the broader your
  expertise, the larger the space you have in which to play: to
  explore and to solve problems.

- **Creative attitude**: This is your talent, or how flexibly
  and imaginatively you approach problems. For example,
  a bioscience researcher who is happy to disagree with
  colleagues is more likely to find innovative solutions. It

will also help if he or she has the ability to be doggedly determined. You are born with talent. But you can maximise it by examining and developing how flexibly and doggedly you tackle problems.

■ **Motivation:** This is how passionate you are to be creative. Skill and attitude are an individual's resources for coming up with new ideas. Motivation determines what he or she will actually **do**.[11]

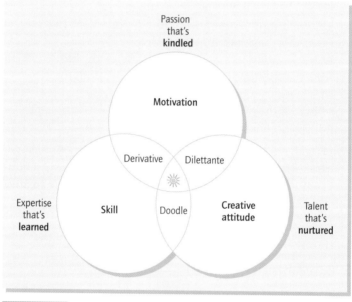

| figure 4.2 | The three crucial elements that all good creative businesses encourage in their people |

■ **Derivative** Motivation + skill produces derivative work – products and services based on other people's ideas. For example, think of those endless, clichéd Hollywood films you've sat through each summer or some of the songs and artists produced by *X-Factor*-type TV shows. Lots of motivation, lots of skill, but the end product is truly tedious because of a lack of creativity. The end product fails to move you emotionally.

- **Dilettante** Motivation + creativity produces interesting work, but it'll be amateurish by comparison to those who have achieved mastery of a particular domain. Dilettantes are creative in their spare time. For example, think of those millions of home-made DIY YouTube videos that are intriguing but miss the mark because the production values and storytelling are poor.

- **Doodles** Creativity + skill produces aimless bits and pieces. I once ran a strategy workshop for the whole leadership team of Aardman Animations, which included the world-famous 'claymation' director Nick Park. At the end of the session I asked to see Nick's work pad. He turned it around and showed me the most incredible doodles of his famous characters: Wallace & Gromit. To transform doodles into the sort of Academy Award and box office success the Wallace & Gromit films enjoyed, you need to add motivation to spend countless hours on the hard work of creative production.

When skill, motivation and creative attitude are brought together – at the centre of Figure 4.2 – an individual will operate in a business environment to the peak of their abilities to deliver creative and innovative ideas.[12]

Inner and outer motivation

Not all motivation is created equal. There are two types:

1 **Carrots and sticks motivation**: This is what psychologists call **extrinsic** motivation because it comes from outside a person. It is the motivation driven from what your business can do to bribe or threaten you. There are lots of carrots: promotion, higher wages, bonus payments, stock options – and various perks from a better office to a boarding card for the company jet. The sticks are familiar too: disdain, demotion and dismissal.

2 **Inner motivation**: This is called **intrinsic** motivation because it comes from inside a person. It's the individual's innate passion for certain activities and challenges. CEO of Yahoo! Marissa Mayer once said: 'Geeks are people who love

something so much that all the details matter'. It is vital, of course, because it's the difference between loving or hating your job.

Enormous amounts of time and money are expended to motivate employees to be creative. Sadly, much of it is wasted because traditional management thinking is obsessed with carrots and sticks. Extrinsic, external motivation doesn't prevent people from being creative; but above a certain level it doesn't help either. It can't prompt people to be passionate about their work; but it can lead them to feel bribed or controlled. This isn't an opinion, by the way. It's fact. It's been established beyond doubt through multiple and robust psychological experiments over many years.[13] People drawn to creative fields are driven by a higher purpose than money: challenge, learning, achievement and peer recognition.

So, encouraging inner motivation is far more successful in delivering creativity. Nobody wants to be a starving artist. And you do need to pay a certain level of remuneration: market rates or, ideally, slightly above. Essentially, you need to take the issue of personal finance 'off the table'. At that point, the research shows the link between cash paid and creativity delivered is broken.

☀ Intrinsic – or inner – motivation is a complex mixture of a person's interests and the environment in which they work.

Reward timing

External rewards can work – and timing plays a big part in how much. Management author Daniel H. Pink distinguishes between what he calls 'if, then' rewards and 'now, then' rewards:

- **If, then rewards** – **If** you do this, **then** you will be rewarded by the company: these guaranteed performance-linked bonuses are less effective as people take them for granted and game the system in order to receive them – ironically, crowding out the naturally occurring intrinsic motivation.

- **Now, then rewards** – **Now** you've performed well, **then** there will be a reward: this is the unexpected treat, such as taking your team out for dinner at the end of an assignment. It works well for creativity as it does not get in the way of a person's intrinsic motivation to be creative.

Too much money reduces creativity

Psychological research stretching back to the 1930s clearly demonstrates, above a certain level, carrots not only don't work, they actually **reduce** the urge to be creative. Pink argues: 'For artists, scientists, inventors, schoolchildren, and the rest of us, intrinsic motivation – the drive to do something because it is interesting challenging, and absorbing – is essential for high levels of creativity. As the economy moves toward more right-brain, conceptual work...this might be the most alarming gap between what science knows and what business does.'[14]

As well as reducing creativity, carrots and sticks have other deadly flaws. They can:

- diminish performance;
- crowd out good behaviour;
- encourage cheating, shortcuts and unethical behaviour;
- become addictive;
- foster short-term thinking.

'If, then', external motivation works well for people in repetitive, process-driven jobs, when the work is what psychologists call **algorithmic** – that's when tasks are routine, mechanical and have a certain obvious logic to them (jobs like picking raspberries, stuffing envelopes or making sales calls. Carrots then offer a route to boosting performance and application. But the best way to reward creativity is with a fair basic salary, with great health care and other benefits, which help to remove unnecessary distractions, and intelligently applied 'now, then' rewards. These rewards can range from a box of doughnuts or a few rounds of drinks to a special night out or a weekend away – or something even bigger. Using the indisputable findings of psychological researchers in your approach to compensation doesn't just make sense in terms of encouraging the right sort of attitude and behaviour; it's probably cheaper.

Collective rewards

An excessive reliance on cash bonuses can also have other unintended consequences. London Business School management professor Lynda Gratton's research into business innovation hotspots shows creative companies tend to favour collective, rather than individual, rewards for a good reason. Individualised, highly competitive remuneration acts as a roadblock to a collaborative culture. She writes: 'It is clear from the research into hotspots that team-based collective rewards do not themselves encourage cooperation. However, they do have the effect of removing the barrier erected by individualised rewards. In a sense, they are neutral rather than positive.'[15]

☀ Make a note in your diary to spring a surprise on your team at the end of the next big project. If you find it difficult to dream up interesting gifts, find someone in your business that can help. Remember the Christmas present concept: 'It's the thought that counts'.

3 Encourage 24/7 learning

Finance director: "What happens if we invest in developing people and they leave us?"

Managing director: "What happens if we don't – and they stay?"
Anon

Most businesses are not able to corner the talent market, however hard they try. If hiring and motivation are steps one and two in the talent journey, step three is helping a person to learn. Insatiable curiosity is a key element of a creative culture. Founder of the advertising agency Ogilvy & Mather David Ogilvy made learning the bedrock for his company: 'We help them make the best of their talents. We invest an awful lot of time and money in training – perhaps more than any of our competitors.'

After the hit CGI movie *Toy Story* had firmly put Pixar Studios on the map, the leaders Ed Catmull and John Lasseter realised one way to sustain success was to create world-class talent development opportunities. They wanted to help new people and veterans expand their horizons. This was inspired by a famous memo written by Walt Disney 50 years earlier. Disney wrote: 'I think we shouldn't give up until we have found out all we can about how to teach these young [people] ... there are a number of things that could be brought up in these discussions to stir imagination, so that when they get into actual animation, they're not just technicians, but they're actually creative people.'

Catmull and Lasseter got hold of this ancient Disney memo and the result of their discussions was Pixar University (PU). 'PU's mission is to integrate learning into the lives of Pixar's employees through classes on everything from self-defence to drawing. The company encourages employees to dedicate up to four hours of every single week to their education. Pixar's Randy Nelson, made the founding dean of PU, said: 'The skills we develop are skills we need everywhere in the organisation. Why teach drawing to accountants? Because drawing doesn't just teach people to draw. It teaches them to be observant. There's no company on Earth that wouldn't benefit from having people become more observant.'[16]

☀ Set up a regular monthly creative session where people can come along with their work and new ideas.

At the heart of Pixar is an idea: 'art as a team sport'. In practice this means people are encouraged to share their ideas and accept feedback without worrying about failure. Now the president of Walt Disney and Pixar Animation Studios, Ed Catmull said: 'Everyone at the company will tell you there are no bad ideas at Pixar, even if they don't end up in the movie.' To assess your own development programme, you could do worse than compare its objectives to the collaborative ideal of the Pixar University. Pixar focuses on developing four basic proficiencies in people across the business:

1   **Depth**: A mastery of one area needed by the business – anything from drawing to the complex programming required to make a Pixar movie. This is the 'skill' element highlighted in the section on motivation above.

2   **Breadth**: A wide array of experiences and interests that give you the ability to explore things from different perspectives. This is about developing a creative attitude.

3   **Communication**: The ability to truly listen; as well as to focus on the person across the table to make sure feedback has been truly heard.

4   **Collaboration**: The ability to respond to others' ideas with 'yes, and ...' rather than 'no, that won't work' or 'this is better'. The 'yes, and' approach is practised in many creative businesses, including the British-based advertising agency Saatchi & Saatchi.

☀ Walt Disney used to say each person in the company has to be able to 'plus' the ideas of others to the make them bigger and better. Plussing ideas and a 'yes, and' approach are both in the spirit of this book's central idea: electric conversations.

Pixar people are encouraged to be emotionally secure enough to make those around them look good. The company believes that their ideas – wonderful stories – will only come to life in the hands of interested people. They value this quality of **being interested** over merely being **interesting**. Interested people want to ask another question, to go even further to get to the best solution, to stay all night to make a project happen. It's a trait, of course, of being intrinsically motivated.

☀ Here are some good questions for the people running your learning programmes:

■ Are we seeking to create a 'learning habit' in our people?

■ Do our programmes cover creative business **necessities**, such as mastery of key skills, developing a creative attitude, communication, collaboration and the creative process?

■ Are our training and development programmes aligned with our strategy? Will they help us to become a more creative and innovative organisation?

It's about attitude

People development is not just about skills and knowledge – it's about attitude. And attitudes start from the top. This was something Alessandro Carlucci, the CEO of Brazil's Natura Cosméticos, realised after the business floated on the stock market in 2004. Carlucci faced a massive challenge: the whole future of the company was being threatened by the competing agendas of senior managers. His solution was to reorganise the executive committee, unify the team around shared goals and explicitly ask them to stop the turf wars.

☀ A cheap alternative, or adjunct, to classroom-based learning is the mentoring of new employees by more senior executives. Research shows that mentoring has a positive impact on performance as well as encouraging a cooperative mindset.[17]

To help them see the bigger picture, each executive was asked to commit to self-development – to embark on a personal journey with an external coach. Carlucci explains: 'It's a different type of coaching. It's not just talking about your boss or subordinates but talking about a person's life history, with their families; it is more holistic, broader, integrating all the different roles of the human being.' One of the senior executives involved, Roberto Pedote, Natura's senior vice-president for finance, IT and legal affairs, said: 'I think that the main point is that we are making ourselves vulnerable, showing that we are not supermen, that we have failures; that we are afraid of some things and don't have all the answers.'

☀ 24/7 learning goes further than paint-by-numbers development approaches. It is about inspiring a prevailing attitude that every brief, project and meeting is an opportunity to learn something new.

Six years after the flotation, Natura Cosméticos grew by 21 per cent in a single year. To encourage the collaborative mindset more widely, coaching was also offered to Natura managers.[18] Carlucci asked everybody to work together to make something bigger and better than their individual fiefdoms.

☀ Encourage 24/7 learning. Blend different
strands together including on-the-job development,
group programmes, coaching, appraisals, 360-degree
feedback, psychometric assessments and interactive
online resources

4 Retain the brightest sparks

Think of this: for every employee who leaves, it costs about 12–18
months of their annual salary to replace them. The reason it is
so expensive is that the business is hit with a tsunami of paper-
work and time to say goodbye to the leaver; as well as recruiting,
onboarding and development costs for the person coming in.
Meanwhile, harassed managers spend valuable time juggling the
transition and unfamiliar work patterns. The worst outcome is if
the gap in experience and talent caused by the departure of a key
person causes quality to fall and creates unhappy customers.[19]

Retaining the right people is always a core capability for a talent-
driven business. You need to strike a balance between challenge
and support.

- **Too challenging**: Even the best people will burn out and leave.
- **Too supportive**: And the best people may still leave – because
  they don't feel stretched. Those people who are left are happy
  to coast. They may have lost all passion for the work and have
  become stale and uncreative. Ironically, these are the people
  who would benefit most from a new challenge; but they stick
  around. After all, nobody likes to get out of a warm bath.

You need to hold on to the best people, those of most value to
your business. The global management consultancy Hay Group
warns businesses face a talent exodus as the global economy
recovers. So, why will talent stick around in your company?

☀ Hold on to your brightest sparks by keeping
them fresh and challenged. Diary a six-monthly or
yearly reshuffle to rotate good people on to new
jobs or high-profile projects.

Design challenging jobs

A study of 20,000 employees asked: 'Why do you stay in your job?'[20] Guess what? 'My wage packet' or 'Getting a raise' didn't make it into the top six most popular replies. The prime reason to stay in a role was 'job-interest alignment'.[21] Translated from HR speak, that means people tend to stay if they're offered a challenging and interesting job with sufficient opportunities for learning and development – as well as a close match between their capabilities and what they are being asked to do. They also want to be empowered with sufficient authority to match their responsibilities.[22] Key factors in numerous staff retention studies are:

- **Confidence in the quality of management**: Your employees must view the business as being well managed - and heading in the right direction.

- **Quality of co-workers**: People want to feel they are working with good people (at least as good as they are).

- **An environment for success**: Processes must allow them to perform – red tape mustn't get in their way.

- **Collegial work environment**: Not surprisingly, people love working in a culture in which they are respected and allowed to work collaboratively with others.

While financial compensation doesn't figure in the reasons to **stay**, it does come out as the number one reason to **leave**, presumably for a company that isn't taking advantage of them. Fairness is the key: people need to feel there is at least a reasonable exchange taking place between what they are asked to put in and what they are allowed to take out.

※ Match people with the right challenging job at the right time in their development. It helps to achieve a psychological personal state of flow, which is a proven way to boost happiness at work (flow is explained in Habit 1: Start an electric conversation).

5 Operate like a sports team

When the HR team at Netflix uploaded a simple PowerPoint document explaining the company's revolutionary talent management policies, they probably didn't expect the slides to be downloaded more than 5 million times. There's a good reason for all the interest: the US provider of on-demand internet streaming media has enjoyed spectacular creative and commercial success. In 2013 alone the company's stock price more than tripled and its US subscriber base grew to nearly 29 million.[23] Netflix tries to hire the best, like anyone else. But, unlike other companies, it also practises a policy of 'tough love', which the founder and CEO Reed Hastings describes as: 'Adequate performance gets a generous severance package'. In other words: deliver the goods, or you're out.

Hastings asks managers regularly to use the 'Keeper Test'. This is one of the questions: 'Which of my people, if they told me they were leaving in two months for a similar job at a peer company, would I fight hard to keep at Netflix?' Employees are also encouraged periodically to ask their manager a potentially awkward question: 'If I told you I was leaving, how hard would you work to change my mind to stay at Netflix?' Netflix is manic about high performance: it estimates in routine procedural work the best people are twice as good as average people. In creative work it finds the best are ten times better than average.

☀ Research at Netflix shows in creative work the best people are ten times more effective than average performers. Try the 'Keeper Test' for the people on your team: where should your retention efforts be focussed?

Netflix doesn't operate a formal annual review process, arguing it is awkward and ritualistic. It also banished the concept of performance improvement plans because they're dishonest. I have to agree. In many companies, I've observed that performance management is not a genuine way to improve performance at all. At that stage the relationship has broken down. It's an unsubtle euphemism: for 'You're on the way to the exit – we're just covering our asses from a legal perspective.' Netflix prefers to encourage managers to monitor performance as part of their week-to-week job. Former chief talent officer Patty McCord writes: 'We asked managers and employees to have conversations about performance as an organic part of their work. In many functions – sales, engineering, product development – it's fairly obvious how well people are doing.'[24]

Innovative businesses have to tolerate a little slack: it's essential for creativity. But that doesn't mean they have to put up with low performance. Employees need to be talented, motivated **and** performing at the highest level. Manchester United is the most successful team in English football, having won more trophies than any other club. The manager doesn't hold an annual review with players at the end of the season. He monitors a player's performance minute-by-minute throughout a match. If the player is struggling, he's substituted immediately. If he continues to fall off the pace required for a world-class team, he'll be dropped from the squad and sold on. United also don't tolerate anyone who thinks they are bigger than the club. They regularly move on brilliantly gifted players if they fail to play for the good of the team. Excellence is the currency of a creative business. A creative business aspiring to sustained excellence can't operate like a family; it needs to operate like a world-class professional sports team.

※ Keep things simple: monitor how well people are doing every week; if they're not performing, have an honest conversation to get them back on track. If this doesn't work, arrange a win-win exit with fair support from the business. Building pointless time-consuming rituals around managing performance doesn't improve it.

Of course time increments are different in business and sport. A 90-minute game might mean a 3-month period in business. And of course you do need to show loyalty to people; as much loyalty as you expect back. If one of your stars goes through a bad patch, you need to stick with him or her to work out if they can be a star again in your environment. Just as if your business went through a temporary dip, you would expect employees to stick around for a while before leaving. But employee loyalty and hard work are not enough. In a creative business it's foolish to measure people on how long they've been an employee or how many evenings or weekends they work. Measure them on ideas and results.

☀ Make two things clear:

1 Creative businesses are fun, exciting and rewarding places to work.

2 The flipside is you need to be high performers to stay on the team.

Electric conclusion

Better talent = better ideas. It's a defining characteristic of a creative business. You need to work like a scout for a major sports club. A talent impresario has to accept it is a huge part of their job. Create a talent journey that entices, motivates, develops and retains the most talented people around – and then demand high performance.

Sparks to remember

▸ Creative leaders develop an obsession with spotting, hiring, developing and retaining the best talent available.

▸ Hiring is important for creative businesses because of the need for new people to bring in ideas, attitudes and ways of doing things.

▸ A creative person must possess a depth of skill and a creative attitude. It is your job to help foster their intrinsic motivation.

▸ Creative businesses develop a culture of 24/7 learning – **learning everywhere, all the time, for everyone**.

▸ In order to retain the brightest sparks, design jobs that are challenging and a good fit for an employee's capabilities.

▸ A creative business can't operate like a family; it needs to operate like a world-class sports team.

CLEAR steps to change

Communicate

List the three people who would cause you a sleepless night if they even thought about leaving. Arrange to chat with them to find out if they feel challenged, if they are learning and developing and what their plans are in the business for the next six months.

Sit down with some key people and brainstorm the key skills, the important attitudes and most impactful outcomes for your learning programmes. In the same meeting think of the cost-free ways you can encourage 24/7 learning: end of project reviews, ideas meetings and mentoring, for example.

Learn

How do you hire currently? What is the process and criteria for finding people with the right attitude, expertise and inner motivation to break the rules'? Look at the last three people you hired – did you make the right decision? How could you do things better?

How do you seek to motivate and remunerate people? What proportion of your talent investment is in basic salary, bonus, perks – and do you have a pot of money for 'If, then' rewards? Can you reallocate a proportion of the 'if, then' rewards to be 'now, then' rewards to drive intrinsic motivation and creativity?

Which projects in your portfolio are the ones that everyone wants to work on? How can you ensure the right talent gets on the right projects to spark creativity? Which customer work bores everyone stiff? How can you get rid of it? What would that cost you (is it a risk worth taking)?

Energise

Redesign how your learning and development budget is being spent.

If required, redesign your reward system to spend more time and effort on encouraging intrinsic motivation.

Act

- Focus your learning programme to achieve higher levels of creativity and innovation.

- Transform your reward system based on what we now know about the balance between extrinsic and intrinsic motivation.

- Assess if your performance and appraisal system uses 'tough love' to keep your talent at the top of their game.

Warning: These actions are fundamental, so be careful about undertaking them at the same time. If you are nervous, or simply don't have the power to do this because you are lower down in the organisation, look to cherry pick and introduce smaller, high-profile tactics that send a message about how highly you value people and their development.

Respond

After 6 months and 12 months, review the outcomes of these programmes. Are you seeing different behaviours and higher levels of learning and performance? If not, go back to the drawing board.

5

Know *why* you do what you do
How to find an inspiring business purpose

You'll learn:

- Why a higher purpose – beyond profit – is vital for business creativity
- The three different types of business purpose
- Why purpose should infuse everything – from company direction to project objectives – to keep people inspired and focused

"To dare is to lose one's footing momentarily. Not to dare is to lose oneself."
Søren Kierkegaard, Danish philosopher

In September 1962 a young president electrified the USA when he proclaimed: 'We choose to go to the Moon in this decade and do the other things, not because they are easy, but because they are hard.' A few months later, John F. Kennedy was visiting the newly built space port in Florida, which bears his name today. He was introduced to three janitors. Kennedy interrupted the trio cleaning a restroom to ask them what they were doing. The first janitor growled: 'What do you think I'm doing? I'm stuck here cleaning toilets.' A bit more enthusiastically, the second janitor, said: 'I'm doing my job. This job feeds my family.' The third janitor, filled with genuine passion, pulled his shoulders back, looked Kennedy square in the eye, and said: 'Mr President, I'm helping to put a man on the Moon!'

As you've probably guessed, this is an apocryphal story. But what's true is Kennedy knew the symbolic value of imbuing projects with inspiring purpose. He knew challenging the US people at that pivotal moment in history was the right thing to do. And it worked. It had a galvanising effect on the nation (and NASA scientists) not dissimilar to the third janitor. Seven years after Kennedy's famous speech, Neil Armstrong became the first human being to walk on the lunar surface. One small step for man, one giant leap for mankind.

Business and the meaning of life

"Purpose must be deliberately conceived and chosen, and then pursued."
Clayton Christensen, innovation guru[1]

This habit is about how, and why, you should discover, clarify and explain the purpose that drives your business. Purpose is the most philosophical concept in commercial life – and the most powerful. It's important because it's **why** you do what you do. It's the simple response to the question: 'Why does your company exist?' The answer to this query, or lack of it, is directly linked to how people feel about your business or team. In harness with your values, the response will decide how much passion, energy and creativity employees invest each day. It translates into a powerful motivator that's stronger than a sense of duty or even a pay packet. It's why people – just like the apocryphal third janitor – want to get out of bed on a cold Monday morning and come to work.

✴ Purpose is not what you're paid for; it's what you're inspired by.

Awkward question: 'Why do you exist?'

Your purpose is your 'Why?' Whenever I'm invited into a company, one of the first questions I ask is:' Why does your business exist?' It's a simple question but, as I've discovered, difficult to answer simply. It normally prompts an awkward silence before people engage with its importance. With luck, it cuts to the chase of what the business is all about. After endless pencil chewing and rewrites, the business' purpose emerges. This is more about self discovery than creativity: you would hope the purpose was lurking there all along. Here are three generic replies to the 'Why do you exist?' question that I've heard a lot:

1 We are here to make money for shareholders.

2 We are here for our stakeholders.

3 We are here to make the world a better place.

We are here to make money for shareholders

Until the early 1990s, if you asked pretty much anyone: 'Why does your business exist?', the response would be: 'Duh, what have you been smoking? To make money, stupid.' The profit motive – called shareholder value by business school boffins – reigned supreme. Anything else was seen as pathetically liberal, hippy and probably disastrously loss-making. Shareholder value was pronounced upon in media interviews by FTSE 100 CEOs and obsessed over in boardrooms across the world. It was also taught as gospel at top business schools. I know this from personal experience. I studied for my MBA at London Business School in the late 1990s and went back to found the Centre for Creative Business within the School in 2004. During my MBA, London Business School treated me and my fellow students to Harvard Business Review case studies. One told the story of a profit machine called Enron, focusing on the energy company's hyper competitive culture. I recently searched for the Enron case study. Not surprisingly, considering the company's ignominious collapse less than 18 months later, that case study has been quietly withdrawn from circulation.

As it turned out, the moral and financial bankruptcy of Enron and Worldcom in the early part of the century were just the warm-up act. As we all know, shareholder value as an organising idea for how to do business has hit a few major problems in recent years in the form of the global financial crash. The meltdown was precipitated in no small part by the high priests of the shareholder religion – investment banks. The cost of mopping up after the world financial crisis has come to £7.12 trillion – a £1,779 bill for every man, woman and child on the planet.[2] Much of what went wrong can be traced back to what those happy-go-lucky investment bankers perceived their business purpose to be: the idea that business is here to make money only in the short term, whatever the long-term cost to society. This idea came close to bankrupting the entire planet.

This fall from grace for the pleasing simplicity of shareholder value has provoked some serious soul searching. Governments, the media, the public, and even some of those in the City of London and on Wall Street, have been asking: 'Why do banks, business and capitalism exist?' An example of how the ground has shifted can be gauged by Barclay's actions since the crash. In 2012, the British bank rewrote its purpose statement as part of 'Transform' – its cultural renewal programme.[3] Barclays pronounced it was here for: 'Helping people achieve their ambitions – **in the right way.**' A distinct shuffling away from a shareholder value purpose to one linked to the welfare of the wider world.

There's no doubt rampant creativity has been unshackled over the centuries, in part driven forward by the profit motive. In the late 1990s, thanks to deregulation and other factors, there was an exuberant burst of creativity in the City of London and other financial centres. Complex financial instruments were invented and refined – derivative, options, warrants, swaps. But, as we've found to our cost, a significant portion of this creativity was self-serving, greedy and short-term. Occasionally it was downright dishonest; conjuring 'value' that never existed.

Being profitable in the long term is obligatory for all businesses. But focusing exclusively on short-term profit does not fire commitment or creativity in people. If the purpose of a business is blind to the needs of the wider world, someone, at some point, will have to pay the piper. Pure creativity often makes people very rich (just ask J.K. Rowling), but it's not the reason why people are creative in the first place. From John Harrison obsessively refining his groundbreaking 18th-century sea clock; the Wright Brothers taking flight; and a young Bill Gates writing computer code; none of these great inventors and innovators were solely driven by the bottom line. Sir John Hegarty, founder of the global advertising agency Bartle Bogle Hegarty, puts it this way: 'Creativity is not an occupation, it's a preoccupation.' If you want a business in which ideas break the mould **in a good way**, it's highly unlikely the motivating purpose will be just about money.

☀ Money motivates neither the best people, nor the best in people. Purpose does.[4]

We are here for our stakeholders

A stakeholder value purpose is focused outside your business – in the rest of the world. It's the philosophy that businesses are here to provide value and livelihoods to a wider group of people beyond those that own the shares: employees, customers, suppliers and the community as a whole. The UK supermarket chain Tesco, for example, states it is here 'to create value for customers to earn their lifetime loyalty'. At some point, a stakeholder purpose – aimed at employees and customers – becomes something a little grander. Some teeter on the edge between being a save the world clarion call and a stakeholder value purpose. Take the BBC's famous mission: 'To enrich people's lives with programmes and services that inform, educate and entertain' or IKEA's motto: 'To create a better everyday life for the many people.' You can hear in these words the original authors had become evangelical about making a contribution to the world.

We are here to make the world a better place

A purpose that focuses upon a higher ideal is an attempt to inspire. Here, businesses have the temerity to reach for the stars and break the perception of being self-serving profit-maximisers; they aspire to be purpose maximisers. Larry Page, co-founder of Google, argues that you should: 'make sure everybody in the company has great opportunities, has a meaningful impact and are contributing to the good of society'. And Page, with his fellow founder Sergey Brin, have made not one, but two, purpose statements famous. The unofficial Google motto is 'Don't be evil', which came from some notes taken during an early discussion around company values in 2000. The official company purpose statement is: 'To organise the world's information and make it universally accessible and useful.' Here are some examples from other businesses and organisations attempting to inspire:

- **International Olympic Committee**: Contribute to building a better world through sport.
- **Disney**: To make people happy.
- **3M**: Perpetual quest to solve unsolved problems.
- **Virgin**: Business as a force for good.

Some purpose statements defy categorisation. One of my personal favourites is Nike's: 'To experience the emotion of competition, winning, and crushing competitors.' This will repel some people but inspire others. It helps to position Nike firmly in the hyper-competitive sports world in which it has been so successful. It also differentiates Nike as an employer, saying: 'We don't want to attract all types of people; but we want to be **loved** by some.'

To encourage electric conversations a **genuine** higher purpose beats shareholder value every time. Apple's Steve Jobs went one better than Larry Page and Sergey Brin when he said famously: 'We're here to put a dent in the universe. Otherwise, why else even be here?' When Jobs and his small team designed the original Macintosh, in the early 1980s, he urged them to make it 'insanely great'. He never spoke of profit maximisation or cost trade-offs. At his first retreat with the Macintosh team, he began by writing a maxim on the whiteboard: 'Don't compromise.' He followed up with: 'Don't worry about the price, just specify the computer's abilities.' The machine that resulted cost too much and led to Job's ousting from Apple. Even Saint Steve got it wrong from time to time.

But the Mac and its descendants undeniably put a dent in the commercial universe. In the end he got the balance right, going on to oversee the development of a string of smash hit innovative products such as the iPad and the iPhone[5]:

☀ Focus on great quality products, and make a genuine contribution to the world, and profits will follow.

I have never yet worked with a successful creative business that focuses purely on profit. A stakeholder purpose is vital for a creative business. The problem is, on its own, it can be seen as merely pragmatic, rather than inspiring. Instead of making it their sole purpose my clients often mould this essential stakeholder duty to employees, customers, suppliers and the general population into a wider business philosophy and culture. In my role as critical friend and change consultant, I unashamedly nudge leadership teams to uncover an aspirational higher purpose: a pithy statement, which briefly describes what the company can contribute to the world. It's the **big idea** customers can rally around, and employees can keep in the back of their mind on those cold Monday mornings when you just want to stay in bed.

☀ What's the inspiring flag you want to rally around? Write your business purpose in one or two sentences. People are magnetically drawn towards a higher purpose – and they appreciate brevity!

A creative purpose: When the world zigs, zag

When you enter the London HQ of the ad agency Bartle Bogle Hegarty (BBH), there are sheep everywhere. Sheep stencilled on glass, sheep made from ceramics, sheep on desks. There is even a life-sized stuffed sheep in the office of the company co-founder, Sir John Hegarty. BBH's iconic image – a black sheep going one way while hundreds of white sheep walk in the opposite direction – speaks volumes about their business purpose: 'When the world zigs, zag.'

A staff booklet, derived from the thoughts of BBH's co-founders John Hegarty, John Bartle and Nigel Bogle, explains the zig-zag idea in more detail: 'If there was one sentence that defines BBH, this would be it. It comes from the first print ad we produced for Levi's in 1982. Zagging is our way of thinking and acting. It means challenging convention, questioning the status quo, finding new answers, new solutions. Zagging isn't about being contrary for the sake of it. We believe differences create space, and space creates opportunity for growth.' [6]

BBH is a great example of how a creative outfit offers meaning and purpose to what they do by elevating the sheer importance of human imagination. One of their beliefs is: 'All roads lead to the work.' They expand upon this as follows: 'Our business model depends entirely on the quality of the work we produce. If the work is working: building fame, reputation and sales for our Clients then we attract more business and so our business grows too. So we need a culture across the whole company that believes in creativity. That supports it, nurtures it, defends, respects and champions it.' This obsession with the importance of the work can take colourful forms. Rose Arnold, deputy executive creative director, BBH London, had the nerve and tenacity to handcuff herself to a client on a pub crawl. She wouldn't let him go until the client had bought the idea the agency was trying to sell. Purpose works in mysterious ways.

When purpose goes wrong

All businesses have to hold their nerve when inevitably they prove to be less than perfect in reality. When they fail to live up to their save-the-world pretensions accusations of tax evasion, corruption, child labour or shoddy customer service tend to knock the shine off an idealistic philosophy. But purpose offers clarity and redemption if it is a genuinely held passion. Business is a complicated place. Change tumbles through like the crashing waves around a white-water raft. A purpose is like a North Star – there to guide a business in what it should do, and not do in good times – and when life gets turbulent and complicated.

✳ Don't worry about falling off your pedestal. Fear of failure shouldn't stop you aiming for the stars.

Purpose from top to bottom

"Make no small plans for they have no power to stir the soul."
Niccolo Machiavelli, Italian philosopher (1469–1527)

Purpose weaves its motivational magic in the gut reaction of employees. It creates passion when people just 'get it'. Put yourselves in the shoes of a Wikipedia employee. It's your first day in the online encyclopedia business. As part of your induction, you're asked to have a chat with the founder, Jimmy Wales. Jimmy puts his coffee down, looks you in the eyes, and says: 'Imagine a world in which every single person is given free access to the sum of all human knowledge. That's what we're doing. And we need your help. Our vision is to create and distribute a multilingual free encyclopedia for every single person on the planet in their own language.' Wouldn't that inspire you to try to think of a few good ideas to help?

But employees can't be expected to keep such high-blown concepts front-of-mind every day. Creative businesses need to go further. Purpose needs to be baked into the very bones of the company from top to bottom. It starts with the story of why the business exists, but then needs to be brought back down to earth for every employee. So, how do you successfully land these 20,000-feet ideas – and weave them into the fabric of the everyday life in your business?

To do this creative leaders become experts at seeking out challenging and difficult work: a kind of higher purpose at project level. The trick is then to match the right people with the right projects. This approach is supported by a global survey, which concluded, the more labyrinthine, ambiguous and tough the project, the better in terms of sparking creativity. It turns out that, for higher order jobs, people prefer hard work that makes them think a little.

As well as the enjoyment of creative problem solving, people know harder work will offer opportunities for self-development.

Creative people are more engaged when they feel like the project they are working on is important and will lead to the further growth in their skills. People naturally want to build their capabilities to go on to tackle even more challenging and difficult projects in the future.

※ For creative people 'the work' – and the skill and personal development that results – is often a reward in itself.

Lightning conclusion

Purpose can manifest itself in an infinite number of ways: an eternal quest like Google's mission to sort out all the data on a planet; a challenge like President Kennedy's thrown gauntlet to the US science community; a beguiling, curiosity-fuelling question such as Virgin's 'How can business be a "force for good"?'

But the 'purpose of a purpose' is that it supports everything else that happens in a business. It is a kind of philosophical infrastructure – the load-supporting steel skeleton of your organisation. When you live your business 'why?', your organisation becomes a lightning conductor for electric conversations and the sparks of good ideas.

Sparks to remember

- A purpose is about understanding and clearly communicating the fundamental **why?** your business exists.

- In combination with other factors, business purpose channels the passion, energy and creativity of your employees.

- Creative businesses emphasise the quality of the work and contributing to the world over making money.

- Leaders need to hold their nerve when their business inevitably proves to be less than perfect in living up to their purpose.

- Purpose needs to be baked into the very bones of the company from top to bottom – this is embodied by complex, ambiguous and difficult work.

CLEAR steps to change

Communicate

Discuss your business or team purpose with a group of key people. A purpose is useful only if it gets people talking, thinking and behaving differently.

Learn

What purpose statements inspire you from other organisations you know and respect? How do they speak to you and align with what that business is all about?

Energise

Is there a written purpose statement for your business that's wider than pure: 'We make money'? What is it? What does it mean to you and your people?

Act

If your business doesn't already have a purpose statement, write one by yourself or with some team members. Try writing three versions and see how they grab you. Here are some useful questions guaranteed to create some sparks:

- What problem are we fixing?
- Who are our key stakeholders?
- How are we 'saving the world'?

I have helped teams and departments create their own purpose statement within the context of a larger business. So, all of the above exercises can help if you are running a smaller part of a larger company.

- Purpose from top-to-bottom: Make a list of your key people and find out who needs to be allocated to a challenging, purposeful project to spark their creativity.

Respond

After you have created a new purpose statement – or dug into an existing one – take it further. How does your purpose impact on what your business or team should be focusing upon this year? What should you start doing more of – or stop doing completely?

6

Connect through shared values
How to inspire passion in your people

You'll learn:

- How to develop shared business values to forge an emotional bond with employees
- How values equal business personality, which leads to commitment and creativity
- How to develop values linked to purpose, strategy and employee behaviours
- How to avoid the 'say-do' gap, corporate frisbees and meaningless platitudes

"Those are my principles, and if you don't like them ... well, I have others."
Groucho Marx, comedian (1890–1977)

In 2009 Tham Khai Meng had made his home in a 19th-century firehouse in New York City. He'd moved there from the Far East when the global advertising business Ogilvy & Mather appointed him as worldwide chief creative officer. Appropriately, the firehouse had once been home to another ambitious artist when he first landed in the Big Apple: Andy Warhol.

Khai had been promoted under the new agency leadership of Miles Young who had been selected as CEO in the same year. They made a formidable duo. Khai graduated from Central St Martin's College of Arts and Design in London with first-class honours. He found his way into advertising where he discovered an early aptitude for branding work. He has now been dubbed by the press as: 'One of the world's most influential people in the communication business.' CEO Miles Young was an Oxford graduate who joined Ogilvy in 1982 and was appointed to the UK board just four years later. A colleague said this: 'You know that thing where people say "he's the smartest person in the room"? Miles really is!'

From their shared office at the company's New York HQ, the pair saw a business that had lost its mojo. Just over 60 years after it had been founded by the legendary adman David Ogilvy, the agency was in a serious creative slump. Creative businesses differentiate themselves through reputation - and that's benchmarked by the number of awards they win. At the annual advertising 'Oscars' in Cannes in 2009 Ogilvy & Mather had been conspicuous by its absence from the winner's podium.

Miles and Khai knew they needed to change the culture of the business. The sheer size and geographic scope of Ogilvy – 450 offices in 120 countries with 18,000 employees – made that a significant task. The first thing they did was to jettison the existing 'competency framework'. It wasn't working. The staff in the business just didn't know what it meant to them. There was no practical link, or emotional connection, between the big picture and individual behaviour.

In its place Miles and Khai created a vision of Ogilvy & Mather's future. It embraced the tension at the heart of an ideas business by clarifying the 'Twin Peaks' of ideas and effectiveness. To drive home the importance of creativity to the business, they described what 'pervasive creativity' would look like: everyone in the organisation, regardless of title or department, had to be responsible for creativity in their domain. That included finance, HR and of course at the creative coalface – working on brand campaigns.

Khai said: 'Creative innovation requires a working environment that awakens creativity in everyone in the organisation, encouraging what may seem silly ideas.'[1] The other Twin Peak – effectiveness – was how the business brought research, knowledge, analysis and creativity **together** to 'produce content that sells'. Worldwide effectiveness director Tim Broadbent put it this way: 'The Twin Peaks are the two sides of the same coin. Creativity leads to effectiveness, and focus on effectiveness allows clients to buy highly creative work.'[2]

The Twin Peaks were accompanied by eight 'habits'. This provided agency staff with an important yardstick for their attitude and behaviour at work. It was an attempt to describe the best elements of Ogilvy & Mather's organisational personality. Global talent director Marie-Claire Barker said: 'We linked the eight habits, or personal principles, to the Twin Peaks vision. We didn't want to reject the past so we were careful to honour and build upon the Ogilvy & Mather philosophy personified by David Ogilvy.' The eight habits (or values) were presented to staff in a beautifully designed red handbook: 'The Eternal Pursuit of Unhappiness', as personal virtues – there to crowd out the lure of polar opposite vices.

Virtues	Vices
Courage	Fear
Idealism	Expedience
Curiosity	The status quo
Playfulness	Boring
Candour	Tyranny of politeness
Intuition	Cold arithmetic
Free-spiritedness	Bureaucracy
Persistence	Giving in

Barker added: 'I have a background in fast-moving consumer businesses, where we used to launch big programmes. It doesn't work like that at Ogilvy & Mather. Things get picked up. We don't like to be too directive.' The leadership team knew it was key to the success of the eight habits that individual Ogilvy businesses around the world were allowed to interpret them as they saw fit. Miles Young had worked in many different territories in his long Ogilvy career so he knew intuitively how irritating and counterproductive it was when head office forced new initiatives on regional offices. Young is keenly aware of the importance of people in a creative business: 'We are not primarily in the communications business. O&M is in the talent business,' he says. 'Finding talent, encouraging talent, developing talent – that's my first role before I start to do anything else. It's something I love, all the more so because talented creative people have their own very special needs.'

The intention was for the Twin Peaks and eight habits to be **pulled** by staff rather than **pushed** from leaders. Some behaviours were modelled from the top to begin with. For example, the development of personal objectives for each leader was kicked off by Miles himself. He opened one board meeting by talking openly about his own personal goals. He then turned to each person around the table and asked them to produce their own objectives linked to the agency vision and the habits. They went on to talk to their direct reports about their personal objectives, and presented the same challenge forward. In this way clearly defined behaviour and performance objectives were cascaded through the business.

The transformational 'habits' approach engaged staff on a very personal level. Its aim was to find a set of inspiring and practical shared values with which people could engage. It has been staggeringly successful, as Figure 6.1 shows.

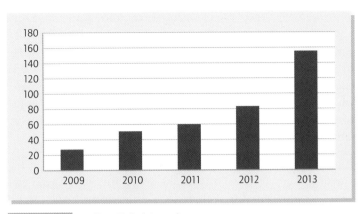

figure 6.1 Ogilvy Global Awards

Four years after Miles and Khai took over, Ogilvy & Mather became the first agency to be awarded over 100 Lions in one year. At the 2013 Cannes Lions Festival the agency also won its first ever Creative Effectiveness Award, as well as being named Network of the Year for the second year in a row. The policies introduced by Miles and Khai to introduce a values-based personality to the business was rewarded with a record-breaking 155 Lions overall across 29 countries, reinforcing their revived creative credentials. Ogilvy was back.[3]

Falling in love

"A business has to be involving, it has to be fun, and it has to exercise your creative instincts."
Richard Branson, founder of Virgin[4]

If people are to bring their heart and soul into the office and raise their head above the parapet to offer new ideas and ways of doing things, the relationship with the business needs to be more than a transactional contract based on a wage slip at the end of the month. It needs to be more than a logical understanding of strategic objectives and their part in that – or even a sense of duty.

More than any other type of organisation on the planet a creative business needs to forge a relationship of trust and empowerment.[5] Relationships are about emotion, connection, and even love. So, this habit is about how you can woo your employees. How you encourage them to fall in love with the idea of your business and what it does, just a little bit. Enough love to forge an emotional connection. People need an emotional connection to take risks, table ideas and start electric conversations.

Stuart Murphy, director of entertainment channels at the TV, broadband and mobile business Sky, sees it this way: 'Each company has a personality. Values are a formal way, I suppose, of saying "this is how our company views life and treats people". Your values need to make sense as a world view, as well as being appealing to customers and people who work there. I've been at places where the values have been very different to people's behaviour. Management thought just by listing them, or writing them on the walls, it would make a difference. This isn't the case. You need people who really believe the values – who are prepared to make the change personally.'[6]

People find it hard to fall in love with a business. They find it easier to fall in love with people. So, it's important to imbue your business with the sort of attributes we normally associate with people: unique ways of thinking about things, preoccupations, passions, a certain recognisable style, attitudes and beliefs. You need your business to get a life – or, at least, a personality. You need your business to have values.

☀ Describe your business as a person. What sort of individual would he or she be? Brave? Efficient? Kind? Offer that person some feedback on his or her strengths and weaknesses. This exercise helps lay the ground work for developing engaging business values.

Values: not for sale

Core values are what the company believes in. Often they can be traced back to the beliefs and attitudes of the founders. They are deeply ingrained principles that guide actions and, crucially, are divorced from the logical, profit-making motive of a business. They require no commercial justification. You don't have values to use in an investment argument with a rich investor from *Dragon's Den*. You have them because they feel right.

Some companies argue that their values are so important they would stand by them, even if they lost money. Ralph S. Larsen, CEO of Johnson & Johnson, put it this way: 'The core values embodied in our credo might be a competitive advantage, but that's not **why** we have them. We have them because they define what we stand for, and we would hold them, even if they became a competitive disadvantage.'[7]

※ Sell your products, not your values.

Values = business personality

Virgin Media employs a chief values officer called Red. Red sits on the executive committee. He has a big profile in the business. When I was working with Virgin Media on a project to refresh the Virgin values, I was based in Red's office for some exploratory interviews. It was explained: 'He's out today.' The office was complete with his personal items, security pass, and a nice view of the forest that surrounds the Virgin Media HQ in Hampshire. I was surprised to see he even has pictures of him holidaying with Sir Richard Branson on Branson's private island.

Red is a puppet. That's not a metaphor for a weak executive controlled by others. He really is a puppet made from furry red material. He was created by Virgin Media to represent the company's values: insatiable curiosity, heartfelt service, delightfully surprising, red hot, smart disruption and *straight up*. Red symbolises Virgin Media's personality and reflects Branson's own entrepreneurial mindset. Red sends all-staff emails and occasionally appears at company events. He's a tangible way for Virgin Media to start a dialogue with staff about how they can engage with and interpret the values.

✳ Work out the most impactful way to bring your business values to life. It doesn't have to be with a furry puppet.

People who believe what you believe

When employees fall a little bit in love with working for your business it's called engagement. Engagement measures a person's positive or negative emotional attachment to his or her business, job, team and colleagues.[8] We fall in love with people, movements, pop bands, and even businesses, when our personal values have some kind of match, a crossover, with that entity. Engagement creates sparks. Studies demonstrate employee engagement plays a central role in translating resources and investment into innovative behaviour. Six out of ten people who report they are engaged by their company say it's this emotional connection that brings out their most creative ideas. The proportion of employees who are unengaged and still have good ideas at work is a measly 3 per cent.[9] Suzie Carr, head of talent, performance and engagement at Virgin Media, puts it this way: 'To us it's all down to discretionary effort. We know from our research engagement drives that, let's face it, that's gold dust.'

The same link between emotional connection and desirable outcomes occurs in the most unlikely places. BAE Systems Plc is a massive British defence, security and aerospace company with operations around the world. Building nuclear submarines and fighting vehicles of all kinds takes a high level of design, creativity and innovation right down to the factory floor. Managers at BAE report that measures to encourage engagement amongst shop floor employees reduced the time taken to build a fighter plane by a quarter.[10]

You'd think in the grip of an economic meltdown touchy-feely concepts like engagement would be quietly shelved. Not true. In 2012, in the depths of a global recession, leaders prioritised engagement ahead of trimming staff costs.[11] Nine out of ten of the world's most admired companies believe efforts to engage employees created competitive advantage.[12] In fact, there is research spanning half a century that demonstrates staff engagement drives peak performance, productivity, low levels of absenteeism, better staff retention, outstanding customer service – and, of course, creativity and electric conversations.

☀ Hire people who believe what you believe.

Engagement will even encourage people to say nice things about your company when they go to the pub. In one business I've worked with, engineers were so ashamed of the company logo they would strip off any identification that linked them to the business before they knocked off for a pint. When the business was bought by another company that valued engagement, their behaviour changed. They were more than happy to advertise who they worked for. Some even made sure they put on a company fleece **before** leaving for a drink. They were proud of the association and wanted other people to know it.

☀ Measure the engagement of your employees and benchmark it from year-to-year as a key performance indicator (KPI).

Health warning: inspirational guidelines, not rules

One of the tricky balances of a creative business is to find people who share your values, who want to buy in to the culture of your business – but are also prepared to challenge the status quo. It is important that values are general principles – what we believe in – but not a behavioural straight jacket, or a one-size-fits-all recipe for corporate robots. The fact values mean slightly different things to different people only enhances the personal connection. There need to be guidelines that can be interpreted with flexibility, latitude and imagination. When values become behavioural rules they kill creativity.

※ Create opportunities to debate your business values with employees. Where values are concerned discussion is always good. Electric conversations about the link between values and behaviours are especially useful.

Values and big picture strategy

It is important to understand how values sit alongside business strategy. Values are about emotional commitment and what the business believes in for all time. Strategy is about rational understanding and how the business copes with the next three to five years. They are not the same thing; but they do support each other.

Strategy is developed by answering the following crucial, big picture questions:

1   Where do we want to go – and what do you need to do differently to get there?

2. How do we compete to achieve our objectives?

The best way to answer these fundamental queries lies in an analysis of your strengths and weaknesses put together with the opportunities and threats in your competitive environment. The answer will be based upon a rational, cause-and-effect argument for how your business is setting objectives (question 1) and choosing to define its unique position in the marketplace (question 2).

To clarify the **where do we want to go** part of core strategy, I work with clients to create a set of clear corporate objectives. A solid, differentiated strategy is vital. It should be the core of any decent business plan or pitch for financial backing. The unique value proposition of your business, department or team is expressed in a blend of products cross-referenced with the customers you serve. With a creative business another important factor is **how you do things** – core competencies – and **what you know** – your unique knowledge base.

☀ Develop strategic objectives for your business or team.

But all this sensible stuff is not enough. It runs into a problem when you need your people to love your business. Strategy takes you to the party; but doesn't encourage anyone to dance. The problem is that most businesses are like Mr Spock from *Star Trek*. They rely solely on the left side of the brain where corporate strategy thinking happens. As a result their pitch to engage employees, is based on sensible, but uninspiring, arguments:

- **Argument 1**: The logic of success through good strategy ('We offer you security and success')

- **Argument 2**: The logic of transactional salary and benefits ('You'll be well paid and looked after if you stick with us').

This is necessary, but not sufficient, to make electric conversations more likely. Creative businesses have to add Captain Kirk's passion to Mr Spock's logic. Creative business needs both.

☀ Seek to bring together the head and the heart of your business when you communicate with your team.

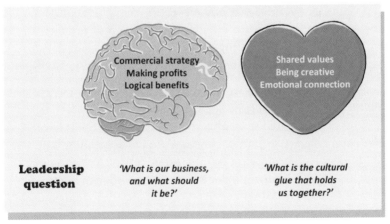

| Leadership question | 'What is our business, and what should it be?' | 'What is the cultural glue that holds us together?' |

figure 6.2   Make sure the head and the heart of your business both get to speak

We need to rebalance our businesses towards the right-hand side of the brain: emotion, passion, feelings, ethics – and creativity. Leaders need to learn to embrace the hard and soft sides of a business' personality. In this way we can ensure organisational culture and behaviours are aligned with the big picture of commercial strategy. I use the thinking model[13] in Figure 6.3 to kick off a strategy development process with boards of directors. It helps when a business is trying to plot its way forward because it recognises the dual importance of left-brain logical strategy and right-brain emotional values. We then use it to get to the nitty gritty of how both strategy *and* values drive culture and behaviours.

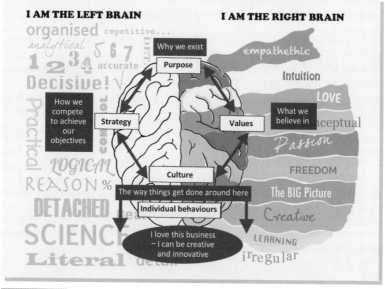

figure 6.3 How strategy and values drive behaviour*

☀ Think about values being equally as important as strategy; not a take-it-or-leave-it device when times are good.

*Based on Campbell, A., 1996. *Mission and management commitment*. Ashridge Strategic Management Centre, March. I have added the concept of culture into the model (as well as behavioural standards), as I found it to be the language of my clients and a useful way to make the intangible 'climate' of a business something that can be influenced and managed.

Finding a point of difference

Since the 1980s, when the strategy guru Michael Porter argued for differentiation as the main strategic focus, companies have been striving to do just that. Clearly it works: Southwest Airlines, Google, Amazon, eBay, Facebook, Pret A Manger and Cirque Du Soleil are all good examples of companies that did spectacularly well by being different. When you offer the market a new value proposition, you change things dramatically. You create a brand-new perceived value and, for a while at least, your business is the only seller.

But it is hard to create acres of clear blue water between your offering and another when a market is mature and standardised in the mind of customers. Take advertising, for example. Most corporate clients are accustomed to what they are buying, what they are looking for and how much it costs. There are differences between agencies, but often they are quite slight. I'm sure at some point a paradigm-busting new strategy for offering value in advertising will emerge. But, in the meantime, it's difficult for agencies to distinguish themselves in a crowded marketplace.

Another challenge to being different is being able to take the required risks. Few executives feel they have the power or bank balance to rip up the rule book. If you are in middle management, or running a business owned by a corporate parent, it's a 'big ask' to place large strategic bets without sign-off from above. But developing a unique culture is another lower risk route to differentiation. And it's especially valuable for businesses striving to be creative because it builds a clear path to attract, retain and motivate talented people who have ideas.

※ Differentiate through your unique creative culture. It's a low-risk way to put clear blue water between yourself and the competition (it's also impossible to copy).

Meaningless values

Wouldn't you like to work for a fast-growing business, named as the most innovative company six years in a row; that had values of integrity, communication, respect and excellence chiselled in marble in the luxurious lobby? That was Enron. But, in 2001, the Texas-based energy business collapsed into bankruptcy and scandal. It was revealed its stellar performance was sustained by institutionalised accounting fraud.[14] So much for integrity.

The 'say-do' gap

Meaningless values written on the walls have no power whatsoever. Authentic values embodied by management and lived by employees can change your commercial future. Authentic company values are shown by who gets rewarded, promoted or fired. Recently there's been a sea-change in how seriously businesses take values. Some of this work to stimulate employees' hunger for engagement has been successful. But problems remain. And anyone who has worked in a business knows exactly what they are: the yawning gap between say and do.[15] This is the difference between what the business preaches, and what it practises. The gap between what you say as a manager, and what you do, eats away at your credibility. There are two types of **say-do** gaps that cause the most trouble:

- **Straight-forward deceit**: Leaders who use values to mask diametrically opposed leadership behaviours; assassinating unwanted employees or cost saving, for example.

- **Insufficient commitment**: Leaders who are corporate box tickers, apathetically ticking off items on the what-we-need-to-do-as-a-good-company form. This is a bit like paying lip-service to corporate social responsibility. Values are hard to implement because you have to match words with deeds. If commitment is not forthcoming, guess what? You get out precisely what you put in. Nothing.

If you are going to have values, they need to be sacrosanct and central to everything. The highly-successful content streaming business Netflix reinforces values in the 360-degree review process as well as hiring, promotions and exits. It asks employees to as act as values police by encouraging them to challenge behaviour inconsistent with their values of judgement, communication, impact, curiosity, innovation, courage, passion, honesty and selflessness.[16]

Corporate frisbees

Management deceit and insufficient commitment means a lot of energy is wasted on corporate frisbees.[17] A new corporate frisbee is created when values are just words on a page and not lived in the business. When the corporate frisbee is thrown – often at a glitzy, razzmatazz event – employees in the trenches look up for a moment, admire its parabolic arc, and then … don't give it another thought. The result: a total waste of time and money. Or worse, the corporate frisbee is viewed as a cynical exercise in pulling the wool over people's eyes while crafty management get on with their real job of slashing budgets, cutting jobs and counting money.

Meaningless platitudes

Occasionally executives tell me: 'Values are pointless; you could apply the same values to any business – they're just platitudes.' I find that's often because the business has confused real values with permission-to-play values: the minimum behavioural standards required of any decent person. We all expect people to show integrity, to have respect for their co-workers and to be honest. But, unless you are putting your own differentiating twist on universal human values, you are not telling a distinct story of what you believe in as a company. It is possible to write differentiating values if you have a distinct enough vision of how you want people to be in the office.

☀ Name the business from its values below. Here's a clue – I've left the same number of Xs that are required to spell their name:

- No cynicism
- Nurturing 'wholesome US values'
- Creativity, dreams, imagination
- Fanatical attention to consistency and detail
- Preservation and control of the XXXXXX magic[18]

Values and profit

Just to prove values are about real profit, and not just tree-hugging blather, here's a salutary tale of a lot of money going West. In the mid-2000s, Tesco was the darling of the UK's food retailing industry: the number one player and very profitable to boot. From its UK stronghold, CEO Sir Terry Leahy took the decision to move decisively into the tempting US market – and the Fresh & Easy supermarket chain was born. Leahy sent his most senior lieutenant, Tim Mason, to run the start-up and Fresh & Easy opened its first outlet in Hemet, California, on 1 November 2007.[19]

The supermarket was to be the first of 1,000 convenience stores that would bring much-admired British retailing to lucky US consumers. Just as the USA's Walmart had bought the Asda chain in the UK; so Tesco would now challenge the US giant in its own backyard. Three booming US states – California, Arizona and Nevada – were picked for the launch. What could go wrong?

As it turned out: a lot. The venture never turned a profit during more than five years of trading. Only 199 stores were opened. After just two years, retail analysts were whispering Tesco had completely misjudged the US market by arrogantly imposing British retail models on a reluctant and conservative US shopper.[20] In April 2013 the new CEO Philip Clarke announced Tesco would be cutting its losses and selling the business. The total cost of this fiasco: £1.2billion.

There were a number of factors involved, but an indisputable point is Tesco failed to understand the needs of US shoppers. Retail consultant Phil Dorrell said: 'Tesco took its eye off the ball in spectacular fashion and, in its goal to be a world-beater, forgot to take care of the basics.'[21] What's this got to do with values? One of Tesco's most cherished values is to 'understand customers better than anyone'. Tesco built its reputation on mining information to know the mind of British shoppers almost better than they did. But US customers were repelled by things UK customers took for granted: stark aisles, plastic-wrapped fruit and vegetables, ready meals and self-service checkouts. The USA is a country where bagging up groceries for struggling shoppers is a customer service essential. Despite deploying serious amounts of customer research, much of the Tesco management team on the west coast were Brits. Tesco fell down on its own core principle of customer insight. The moral of this story: forget your values at your peril; it leads to disaster.

Changing values

It is advisable to treat values as untouchable. It's off-putting when a person's personality seems to change at will. But never say never. The Virgin values mentioned earlier were an update from principles that had served the business well for decades. Sometimes even values need to be updated to stay tuned with what the business is all about. Take IBM, for example. I visited this technology giant in 2011 while delivering a leadership programme for a global TV production company. I was at IBM's innovation hub in Stockholm and I can tell you they take creativity and innovation very seriously indeed. The sheer effort and focus upon generating new ideas speaks for itself. IBM boasts 12 research labs worldwide and has held the record for most patents generated by a company for 20 consecutive years. Its employees have garnered five Nobel Prizes, six Turing Awards, ten National Medals of Technology and five National Medals of Science.

Part of this continuing success may be down to the fact, after 89 years in business, the leaders of IBM decided they needed to change their values. One of the executives I was with told me in awe how they did it, while still gaining buy-in from the majority of staff – well over 400,000 people.

IBM wasn't always that big. It was founded by president Thomas Watson, Sr in 1914 to make tabulating machines, scales for weighing meat and cheese slicers.[22] At the time, Watson decreed three corporate principles called the basic beliefs: *respect for the individual, the best customer service*, and the *pursuit of excellence*. These informed IBM's culture and drove success for decades.

But by the early 1990s the company had been through the most traumatic near-death experience in its history. Under Lou Gerstner 'Big Blue' fought back and transformed itself from a business that made huge mainframe computers into a provider of integrated hardware, networking and software solutions. In 2002, Sam Palmisano took over as CEO and felt the basic beliefs could still serve the company, but needed to be updated into a new set of values that could re-energise employees. Palmisano set about his task with a will. He first discussed it with 300 senior executives, and then opened up the debate through a survey of over 1,000 employees. He tried to get a sense of what people at all levels, functions and locations thought about IBM's values.

Out of this research grew a set of propositions that were fed into a quintessentially IBM communication tool – the 'Values Jam' – a huge online discussion. After – and even during – the jam, company geeks pored over the postings, mining the million-word text for key themes. Finally, a small team that included Palmisano came up with a revised set of corporate values. He announced the new principles to employees in an intranet broadcast in November 2003: '*dedication to every client's success, innovation that matters – for our company* and *for the world, trust* and *personal responsibility in all relationships.*' Like most values, they don't sound earth-shattering from a superficial read. But they are powerful within IBM because they have the legitimate buy-in of all employees.

Lightning conclusion

Values are about emotions, so they are perceived by some managers as 'fluffy stuff best left to HR'. This is not something a creative leader can do. Developing inspiring values, and using their unique ability to connect with the passion of your employees, is vital to success. A match between your business values and the personal values of your employees is the spark that makes a creative culture fizz and crackle with electric conversations.

Sparks to remember

➤ Develop values to drive employee engagement.

➤ The passion in this engagement promotes creativity and discretionary effort.

➤ Hire people who share your values, but also encourage them to challenge the status quo.

➤ Align your commercial strategy and values to create differentiation and drive the right behaviours.

➤ Walk the talk: avoid the say-do gap, corporate frisbees and meaningless platitudes by embodying the business values in your leadership behaviours.

CLEAR steps to change

Communicate

Talk values: find out if your values are understood and relevant for the people in your team, department or business. Who are the people who are at the heart of your company? The people who just 'get it'? If you were producing a poster to explain what the company is all about, who are the guys who would be placed slap bang in the centre of the picture? Talk to them one-to-one and ask them what the company values mean to them.

Learn

Ask yourself, and the people above, the following questions to explore the validity of your values:

- What are the stories people tell in the business when the values were lived – or betrayed?
- What are clear examples of what you do, and what you would never do, as a result of these guiding principles?
- Simple is best: how would you explain your values to a child?[23]

Energise

If you don't currently have written values, write some. Ask the following question and be creative around it: What are the very best – and unique – qualities of your business?

Find the common themes that emerge from this discussion and write them up into a draft set of three to six business values. If you have time, you can then use the questions in the **Learn** step above to test which of these are core values or principles you aspire to.

Act

Develop a clear commercial strategy. Link this strategy to your business purpose from Habit 5 – and your values. Here are some key questions to audit where your strategy is now. Take these questions and lock yourself in a room with some trusted people and don't come out until you have either a good answer for each one or a solid plan to get a good answer.

Unique value proposition

- What is your differentiated position in the marketplace?
- Which one of your customer's problems are you helping to solve?
- What are the trade off and choices you are making (i.e. what are you saying 'no' to)?

Customer relationships

■ Who are you creating values for?

■ Who are your most important customers?

■ How are you establishing and maintaining a relationship with customers that promotes trust and electric conversations?

Capabilities and resources

■ What are the core competencies you need to deliver your unique proposition?

■ What key resources does your unique value proposition require?

Making money

■ What are the most important costs inherent in your business model?

■ For what are your customers really willing to pay?

The questions are straightforward. Having the humility, guts and bravery to look at your business afresh is what's difficult.

Respond

Thinking and acting strategically is not a straight road to a finish line; it's a nerve-ending circuit that you travel around at regular intervals. Live with the clarified values and strategy above for some time and then revisit them again. If they are authentic, the values should not change too much – but you will interpret them differently over time. In today's fast-paced world, expect to change your commercial strategy every two to three years – and make sure you have specific and measurable annual objectives linked to the strategy.

7

Build a business playground
How to electrically charge your creative climate

You'll learn:

- How to lead a culture for business creativity
- How culture drives employee behaviours
- How to boost innovation by removing distractions to play
- How a leader can go about changing culture

"Your brand is your culture."[1]
Tony Hsieh, CEO of the innovate online shoe retailer Zappos

If you drive into a particular valley in southern England, you'll come face-to-face with two, alien-looking domes. The massive structures are owned by a charity called the Eden Project. Standing 50 metres high and well over 100 metres in length, they cover a large area. The entire complex around the domes spreads out to many acres, and is visited all year round by tourists from across the world. Outside, even in summer, the weather in Cornwall can be nippy. Inside the 'biomes' it's very different. They contain the world's climatic and geographic ecosystems in miniature. In the hot, steamy tropical biome, plants such as banana trees, coffee, rubber and giant bamboo jostle for space. Next door, in the Mediterranean biome, visitors are treated to a profusion of temperate and arid plants, such as olives, grapevines, lemon trees and perfumed herbs. This habit is about designing, building and maintaining a business biome in which a creative climate encourages ideas to grow.

What is a creative climate?

You can't order people to be creative. The only levers you have to pull to encourage passion and ingenuity are those that affect the environment in which people work. So, climate – commonly known as culture – is heated up or cooled down by the decisions you make as a leader and manager. Long-term decisions taken around organisational purpose, values and strategy are the environmental structure in which a creative climate develops.

Climate is 'the way things get done around here' on a day-to-day basis. It is the social system in which people work. This is made up of a thousand details: how managers talk and behave, how meetings are run, organisational habits and beliefs, the dress code, office politics, the stories people tell, how staff are paid, who gets a parking pass, who answers to whom, and how performance is rated. Culture is everything that happens in a business – and it teaches people how to think, feel and behave. Your culture is the creative 'temperature' in your biome.

Changing the Sky weather

Let's take a look at how a famous British media company has gone about regulating the thermostat in its cultural biome. Sky was founded by the legendary entrepreneur Rupert Murdoch in 1990. In the two decades that followed, the satellite TV broadcaster turned itself into a British business success story. In a recent instalment of the story, Sky's ambitious leadership team realised it needed to boost creativity in its business culture.

Sky had a difficult birth. This was a truly innovative and groundbreaking pay-TV offering to the British public. Viewers had grown accustomed to two familiar routes for TV to enter their front rooms: an annual, mandatory, licence fee paid to the BBC, and the advertising-funded ITV and Channel 4 for free. At first Sky burned cash at an astonishing rate. Bankruptcy was not out of the question. But, after a rocky beginning, fighting for subscribers, the business established itself as a subversive force in UK media. In time it even became a British institution, building a valuable bridgehead into people's homes, offering them an attractive diet of films and sport – particularly access to the English football premier league.

By 2004, Rupert Murdoch's son, James, had become CEO. In a now legendary speech he caused Sky's share price to plummet when he bullishly announced to a surprised City audience that the business would sign 10 million subscribers by 2010. At the time, Sky had fewer than 7.5 million paying customers. James Murdoch's announcement was seen by sceptical investors as naive optimism: an all-or-nothing-betting-the-farm strategy predicated on growth. Three years later, in 2007, Jeremy Darroch was promoted to CEO and given the job of delivering what he called Murdoch's 'clarion call to action'. And, against the odds, with just 8 weeks of 2010 to spare, the 10-millionth Sky customer was signed.

Darroch is a working-class grammar-school boy from England's gritty North, who had taken an unusual route to the pinnacle of British media. Prior to joining Sky as CEO, he was group finance director at the high-street electrical retailer Dixons; before that he spent 12 years with the consumer goods giant Procter & Gamble.[2] As Sky passed the symbolic 10-million-customer milestone, he admitted 'a sense of relief, and a bit of euphoria'.[3] Along the way he and his team had begun the strategic transformation of Sky from a pay-TV provider into a so-called triple-play business: TV, telephony and mobile. The obvious question was: where would Darroch take the business next?

Sky has always been a business that stayed ahead of the pack through speedy and bold innovation. Darroch knew he needed to continue this constant evolution. It was at this point he had an insight you might not expect from a CEO trained and developed as an accountant. Darroch realised that, although Sky was a formidable technological innovator, and highly commercial, its central purpose was simple and compelling: to entertain people. In the past, the business traditionally had bought a lot of its comedy, drama and entertainment from the USA. After consulting with his team, Darroch resolved to invest hundreds of millions of pounds in home-grown shows to enrich Sky's portfolio. He wanted to set up the business so it had the ability to dream up ideas for hit shows, and then produce them in-house – or commission them from partners. Sky needed to increase the influence of creativity within the business. It needed to be creative for a commercial purpose.

Hiring a catalyst

To help make this vision a reality, Sky hired a young, ex-BBC TV channel controller called Stuart Murphy to shake things up a bit. Murphy is funny, fast-talking and totally focused on creative excellence. He's a ball of energy who laughingly described himself as a 'gobby catalyst' within a few minutes of us first talking on the phone.[4] A fellow Sky executive commented admiringly: 'Some people are drains; Stuart's a radiator. He just emanates energy and creativity.'[5] As head of the business' entertainment channels, Murphy's task was to commission highly creative, original content that would encourage more people to subscribe to Sky – and, importantly, to persuade the 10 million that had already done so, to stick around. He set out to inject more creativity into what was an already well-established business.

His first symbolic act was to move his own desk out of a private office and on to the open floor with his 40-strong team. 'I think an open-plan office really, really helps. Because, as stupid as it sounds, noise helps. It's rare someone will come up with a completed idea on their own. Ideas develop with other people and it's embarrassing doing that in a quiet office,' he said. In his customary informal and self-deprecating style, he added with a grin, 'You also need an awful lot of caffeine!' He then asked all of his managers to follow suit and forgo their private offices. He had a plan for the space that was left. He knocked down the walls between the old executive offices to create large meeting rooms where the team could get together to collaborate and discuss ideas. 'It seems stupid, but the small meeting rooms seemed to be saying we were a small channel; I wanted people to believe the opposite,' he said.

☀ Make an open-plan office part of a wider energetic culture of collaboration – and don't forget to provide quieter areas for people to think and work alone or in small groups.

Changing the physical environment might have been seen as window dressing if it hadn't been part of a larger managerial mind shift. Stuart is unequivocal about how to fundamentally change a business:' It's about developing a creative culture and the attitude of the leadership team,' he asserts. His own creative leadership philosophy is built around dismantling hierarchy and developing a kind environment in which ideas are supported rather than being shot down. He elaborates: 'An idea is a fragile thing. It's a personal thing. That's nerve-wracking; because at work you are amongst people who aren't necessarily friends, they're colleagues. There is no science to say if an idea is good or bad. This means someone can knock your idea down as easily as they can back it. So, creativity is initially quite a flimsy thing. You feel sensitive when you're coming up with an idea. So, a creative environment has to feel kind – kind to ideas.'

But he's clear that a kind culture is not the same as a comfortable culture. Murphy loves Sky because 'we are going a million miles an hour a thousand per cent of the time'. And he admits electric conversations can – and should – involve conflict from time to time. In fact, he describes good creativity as 'spatty' and 'bristly'. He concludes: 'The counterbalance to the non-hierarchical, friendly, authentic, noisy and kind environment is it also has to have structure and focus. You need to know how much money you have to spend coming up with ideas and developing them. You also need to be clear about the reasons why you are being creative – and clearly understand the set parameters and timing needs of a project.'

He is clear that his role as leader is to know when the team needs to focus on creativity and when to focus on delivery, adding:

'That's my job a lot of the time: trying to balance things. It's like this ... people can turn up in a bikini if they want to, but, at the same time, there are also rules on how people behave. When I have screwed up in my job I have got that balance wrong. I have made things too creative or too processy.'

※ Don't worry about the odd argument; do worry if no one ever disagrees. Electric conversations sometimes cause friction. It's the quality of the ideas that counts.

Why is culture so important?

"Our culture is friendly and intense, but if push comes to shove we'll settle for intense."
Jeff Bezos, founder and CEO, Amazon

A wise man one said,' Culture eats strategy for breakfast.'[6] In other words, culture reigns supreme as the heavyweight champ of what will lead to lasting change. You can have a talented and enthusiastic leadership team, a sharp and focused strategy, good processes and excellent products; but, if the company culture is broken or unaligned with the vision, all of this will mean nothing. Bad culture is treacle that companies have to wade through to get to their objectives. Good culture is jet fuel that speeds them on their way. Sir John Hegarty, the creative co-founder of advertising agency Bartle Bogle Hegarty argues it is the context for talented people to excel themselves in your business: 'I'm going to hire someone out of X, Y, Z business. Why is that person going to be better here? The only thing that makes the difference is the culture.'[7]

Culture = behaviour

Culture is important because it drives people's beliefs and behaviours. To understand this link better, let's imagine a person – Sophie – as an iceberg. The tip of Sophie's iceberg, what's observable above the waterline, is her behaviour: what she's doing at work, how she's doing it, her general demeanour. But, like an iceberg, there's plenty going on beneath the surface that we're not aware of. To truly understand Sophie's performance, you need to put on your metaphorical wetsuit and flippers and swim down to take a look below the waterline. There you'll discover Sophie's beliefs and values – the hidden elements of her personality that dictate if she finds meaning and inspiration in the work she does. Sophie's performance in work is influenced heavily by her mental make-up, but also by what management can influence: company culture.

Let's compare two fictitious companies – Outlook Limited and Inspiring Partners – to work out how their cultures affect Sophie's willingness to be creative. Sophie's not a bad employee; in fact she's keen and capable. And, as you can see in Figure 7.1, the personal values she holds dear are 'aim high', 'achieve' and 'work hard'. But, unfortunately the management of Outlook Limited, doesn't value creativity. It is not mentioned in the company's purpose and values – or anywhere else for that matter. Not surprisingly, in this climate, Sophie believes that being creative is risky, and just not worth it.

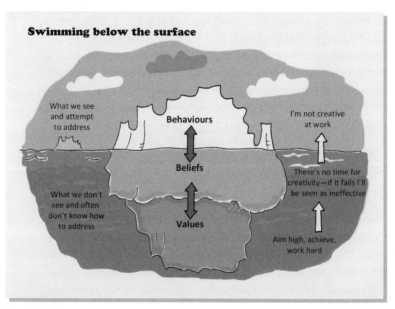

figure 7.1   Sophie and Outlook Limited

When Sophie goes to work at Inspiring Partners, the opposite is true (see Figure 7.2). This business has embraced creativity, managers talk about its importance, and allow time and resources for people to focus on doing things in a creative and innovative way. As a result, Sophie feels able to come up with new ideas – and challenge the status quo every now and then.

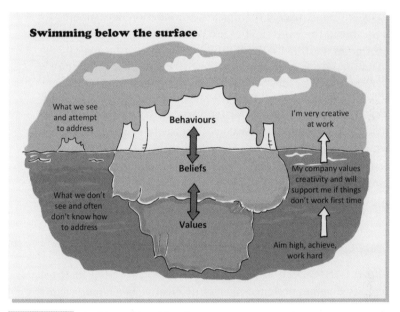

Swimming below the surface

What we see and attempt to address

Behaviours

I'm very creative at work

Beliefs

My company values creativity and will support me if things don't work first time

What we don't see and often don't know how to address

Values

Aim high, achieve, work hard

figure 7.2   Sophie and Inspiring Partners

Sophie holds the same core values in both scenarios. But, because of the differing creative climates in Outlook Limited and Inspiring Partners, she chooses to behave in a different way in different offices. She brings a different appetite for being creative. Her personal values have not changed, but the way Sophie interprets them has.

☀ Encourage your employees to link their personal values to the business' values. It's this connection that drives proactive behaviour and a creative attitude.

Creativity everywhere

Sky's Stuart Murphy is clear that his catalytic creative role would not work if he was not supported by his bosses. He puts a lot of the cultural change at Sky down to the fact that the CEO Jeremy Darroch has built a 'creative cluster of like-minded individuals'. Murphy and others realise that Sky needs this creative climate to extend more widely than just the production department. To help spread the word in 2013, ex-WCRS advertising agency boss Liz Darran was hired as Sky's director of brand and creative.

In her first year, Darran was tasked with rewriting the values of the business. Sky has long been guided by a corporate purpose 'Believe in better'. The phrase represents Sky's restless, entrepreneurial spirit, and is embraced within the business. It embodies what Darran jokingly calls Sky's 'constitutional insurgency': a restless energy that is part of the DNA. Darran jokes: 'We tend to have a failure to sit back and be happy around here!'

☀ **Build a supportive cluster of like-minded individuals around you. It always takes more than one person to change a culture.**

Months of research and internal discussion resulted in three rephrased values designed to electrify creative behaviours: game changing, spine tingling and brilliantly simple. Darran argued that the creation of refreshed values was to offer people some context and meaning for what Sky is all about: 'It's to remind people why they are here. The values have an energy that gives people a different slant; we hope it helps people to be more creative – to think in a different way. It's not about making money. Making money is a result of what we do, not the reason that we do it.' And she made it clear that the values are there to be used and interpreted by staff, to fundamentally change behaviour, commenting: 'It's about flowing these values through to the everyday: for example, what does game changing mean about how we communicate with each other, run a brainstorm or hold a meeting? The values set the agenda and raise the bar for how we behave internally. We hope it leads to more creativity and game-changing behaviour.'

Sky's challenge is to encourage people to re-examine their attitudes in the absence of a tangible threat – this isn't a cultural change forced by a business in trouble. 'The interesting thing for me is how you can build a creative culture, but not from the start-up phase. Sky has grown so quickly it's developed in silos, a bit over here, a bit added over there. That flows over to the physical environment – and the people. It's a patchwork quilt. So, how do you build a culture of creativity back into an organisation that hasn't had that in the first place? My hope is this is ultimately an organisation that has always produced entertainment – so there's innate creativity in here that just needs to be tapped.'

Changing your culture

Changing your culture can be difficult because it is dependent on so many factors. It is like untangling a knotted piece of string:

1 **It is easy not to get it**: Culture is perceived by some as touchy-feely HR fluff involving little more than considerations of office décor.

2 **It is complex**: Culture is connected to all your decisions, large and small, and all the behaviours that stem from those decisions. It is impossible to manage in the traditional sense because it is not something that can be controlled or mandated. Just like a company brand lives in the heads of consumers, not in the marketing department, culture thrives and grows in the minds and behaviours of employees. It can be influenced and lead by the boss – but never manufactured.

3 **It is hard to see**: The prevailing climate is invisible after many years with the business. You become so accustomed to the world being ordered in a certain way that it is difficult to see how it could be different. It is the water that surrounds a goldfish in its bowl: vital, supportive, but hard to see because it has always been there.

4 **It is sometimes owned by people with little motivation to change**: The people who have been with a business the longest – founders or long-serving employees – are often the most senior or influential. So, ironically, the people who have the capacity to change things often can't or won't, because it never occurs to them that things could, or should, be different. It takes bravery and confidence to criticise something you created.

How to untangle it

It is possible to loosen the knot. Otherwise, this would be a dispiriting, and short, habit. To begin proactively developing your business culture, start with the following actions:

- **Value it**: Culture has a reputation for being stubborn to untangle because some managers have failed to grasp where creativity comes from. It needs to be a focus for you. Culture is not at all fluffy. It encourages creativity, which fertilises ideas, which makes innovation possible, which translates into measurable business performance.

- **Become a culture detective**: The attitude and behaviour of managers make the weather in a business climate. By taking care to notice and cherish the right culture you will automatically start to tackle the challenges above. You need to realise that looking after the culture is your job. Take this even further by actively comparing your culture to other organisations. When you're in shops or other offices look for the telltale signs of their culture and ask: 'What can I learn?'

- **Encourage a creative culture**: To boost innovative behaviour remove distractions that prevent play, send a clear message about behaviour with your physical environment and tell good stories – there are more details on these three powerful approaches in the rest of this habit.

☀ Start small. Make it your mission to start at least one electric conversation every day.

Work hard, play hard

"We are all born children. The trick is to remain one."
Pablo Picasso

Have you ever watched children play? They don't do things by half. They're 100 per cent committed to the game. Whether it's make-believe with a dressing-up box, building cities with Minecraft on their PlayStation or playing football in the garden, they live it to the max. Asking them to tear themselves away from that afternoon's current passion is difficult, as any parent will tell you. It's no different when we grow up.

Remove distractions

There is never enough time to keep fit, do the laundry, shop for groceries or look after financial planning. This general lack of time has a knock-on effect at work. It is not possible to be fully engaged, creative and playful if you're trying to block out nagging worries about life's mundane issues or emotional upheavals: securing a dental appointment, sorting out childcare, or wrestling with problems at home. So, if people are your greatest asset, as the old cliché goes, what can you do to help? The question is even more important in a creative business. Many companies have cottoned on to the obvious answer: do as much as possible to remove distractions at work and support people through tough times at home.

SAS to the rescue

An independent US software business has taken this philosophy to the extreme. Based in Cary, North Carolina, SAS began life as a university start-up in 1976. It has grown somewhat since then, and now has 13,000 employees with offices all around the world. Founder Jim Goodnight argues that creative capital is the factor responsible for this success. He passionately believes in an idealised vision for business culture: to treat employees as if they make a big difference. The result, of course, is self-fulfilling: they do.

Goodnight puts his money where his mouth is. SAS employees, and their families, have free access to a massive gymnasium featuring tennis and basketball courts, a weight room and a heated pool. There's also an on-site health care clinic, staffed by doctors, nutritionists, physical therapists and psychologists. On-site counselling is available to help employees to manage the occasional stresses thrown up by the work–life balance. All these services are entirely free. Deeply discounted childcare is also on tap.

Work areas are filled routinely with snacks and treats.[8] SAS even supports employees with adopting a child or arranging a mortgage. Goodnight realises one thing: perks aren't just perks. They are highly symbolic representations of how you value your people. The impressive SAS benefit portfolio exists to remind workers constantly that they're important and that they matter greatly to the success of the firm. It is, of course, a win-win for the business. It frees people from potential distractions so they can stay focused on work.

Lend a hand

Life's random factors will throw a spanner in the works for encouraging creativity. Those standard and traumatising travails – marital strife, drug addiction and health problems – are out of the normal scope of most companies' pastoral care. But, as we all know, they destroy the motivation for creativity, as well as more mundane work-related objectives, such as hitting sales targets and, occasionally, turning up at all. If you are going to help a person to aspire to creativity, you need to lend a hand when life knocks them down. SAS helps people with legal advice to get divorced. The advertising agency Ogilvy & Mather makes a promise to be there for its people through thick and thin: 'We treat our people as human beings. We help them when they are in trouble – with their jobs, with illness, with emotional problems, drugs or alcohol.'

Win-win

It is often debated whether happy workers are more engaged and productive than their discontented counterparts. Or, if organisations that invest in generous practices get rewarded with greater profitability. SAS's performance seems to provide proof that happy, well-supported workers deliver better profits. SAS chalked up 37 consecutive years of record earnings to a high of $2.8 billion in 2012. At the same time, SAS experiences annual staff turnover between 2–3 per cent; compared to an industry average of 22 per cent. The money SAS otherwise would have to spend on head-hunters, training and restoring lost productivity are, effectively, diverted to further enhancing the work–life experience of employees. Goodnight and his team have created a virtuous circle designed to keep the best people inside the business – with their mind on the job.

☀ Encourage people to play at work by removing distractions and lending a hand when they're in trouble. If you get the balance right the investment will pay for itself – and then some.

Physical environment

The physical environment in your workplace can be a negative distraction, too – or a statement of creative intent. We've all visited those offices. Some of us have been unlucky enough to work in them: airless, sterile, carpeted with acres of nylon floor tiles, a few pot plants amid dehumanisingly similar, individual cubicles for worker bees to inhabit. A place where any urge to create something memorable and magical, any rebellious shout would be swallowed instantly in the dismal silence. Sadly, I could be describing a large proportion of work environments in which people spend five days a week – and perhaps a few weekends, too.

Companies dependent on the intellectual capital of their employees are forever looking to spark new ideas inside their walls. Studies of people at work prove conclusively that the office environment – the configuration of desks, the colour of the walls, whether windows provide natural light – can change your mood either positively or negatively. But, surely, we don't need too much evidence to understand this. It stands to reason that, if you want people to stay at work for a long time, to bump into each other, to exchange ideas, to become fascinated, even obsessed, by the projects they are working on, you should make your office fun and comfortable – even inspiring.

Sky's director of brand and creative Liz Darran joined the TV, telephony and mobile company in 2013 'to help encourage creativity everywhere – from the security guard on the front gate to call-centre employees'. As the business developed its thinking on using values to boost creativity, they couldn't help but notice the offices and physical environment didn't quite match their creative aspirations.

As a result, a new south campus has been built, as well as a makeover of the west London offices they inherited from the drug company GlaxoSmithKline. Darran said: 'I don't think it's possible to change a culture without doing something to the physical environment. You need to make a statement. It's not just about "this place makes me happy". It's about a place where you can have certain kinds of meetings: public areas where you can get together to celebrate work, areas where you can present work in a more inspiring way, where you can get together and just throw ideas around.'

Like Sky, savvy businesses across the world have grasped the impact of physical environment and are investing in new ways to make offices playful and energetic:

- Alternative clothing company Comvert transformed an old Milanese cinema into its HQ and built an indoor skateboarding bowl in the space above where the audience used to sit.

- Madrid architecture practice Selgas Cano is submerged halfway underground with views from massive glass windows into the middle of a forest.

- Energy drink company Red converted five pubs in London's Soho into a lounge-like office with a reception that turns into a bar at night.

- Facebook features a mixing desk to practise your DJ-ing skills with plenty of room to skateboard outside.

- YouTube boasts a large putting green in the centre of one of their offices.[9]

As well as promoting fun, your physical environment sends a clear message about expected behaviour:

- **Invent** At Lego in Denmark the colourful, open-plan layout encourages interaction and play between staff to fuel imagination. Light and open meeting rooms are designed to provide a comfortable working environment to turbo charge product development. Everyone is encouraged to play with Lego and come up with something new – and get their work done at the same time.

- **Be yourself** The world's largest online shoe retailer Zappos has built its cultural mantra of individuality into their Las Vegas headquarters. Each employee gets to stamp their own imprint into the office design. They are encouraged to make their own space deeply personal with decorations, toys and trinkets. This means that every cubicle is unique and the office feels less sterile and more enjoyable to work in.

- **Work hard, play hard** At Googleplex in California the generous facilities include a gym, free laundry rooms, two small swimming pools, multiple sand volleyball courts and eighteen cafeterias with diverse menus – all of the food is free. There is a rule at Google that nobody is allowed to be more than 100 metres away from food, so you'll find kitchens everywhere, as well as an appetising cafeteria where every employee is fed three times a day, for free.[10]

- **Collaborate** The mobile operator Dtac recently merged six separate Bangkok offices under one roof, creating the largest ever lease in Thai history, occupying 650,000 square feet. Dtac needs to react very quickly to changing market conditions so its offices enhance the following belief: 'cooperation and communication, strengthen common goals, and increase creativity'. The brand approach is 'play and learn'. This is reflected in a massive circular library, an amphitheatre and an entire floor dedicated to fun, with indoor soccer, table tennis, running track and concert and performance spaces.

If all this sounds a bit extravagant, and you're short on funds, take your inspiration from the charitable fundraising outfit Pallotta

TeamWork based in Los Angeles. Its office makeover was on a strict budget of just $40 per square foot. It customised old shipping containers and transformed them into office space inside a large warehouse. The unique design and fresh colours make for a work environment that's not just cheap to build, but cheap to run.

☀ Send a clear message with your office. It doesn't need to cost the earth – be creative with what you already have.

Investing money in removing distractions, lending a hand and developing a business playground might seem generous. But, as long as you have the financial wherewithal to take a long-term view of business success, and you provide benefits and an environment as part of a wider cultural change, it is sound investment. It becomes a creative business virtuous circle, as shown in Figure 7.3.

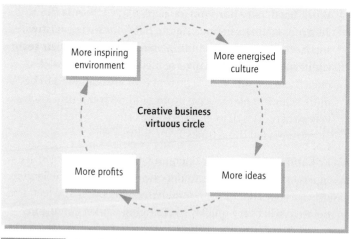

figure 7.3 Creative business virtuous circle

Beware the beanbag fallacy

The playful environments of highly successful companies are an inspiration to all leaders. But be careful of what I call the beanbag fallacy. That's the erroneous idea that office environment has a larger impact on your creative culture than it actually does. It is important, but is just one aspect – a symbol – of your attitude as a business. It doesn't work in isolation. Buying a ping pong table, some brightly coloured seats and applying a few coats of paint should not be the first, or only, thing you do to boost creativity in your business. On its own this won't suddenly create a hot bed of ideas. In fact, unless it's backed up by the other habits in this book it will be quietly derided by staff as a sad, cynical attempt to paper over the cracks. But, in concert with the other habits, building a business playground can make a statement about your business' attitude to hierarchy, creativity and play.

Tell good stories

Culture is made of stories. You can gauge the energy in a company climate by the type of tales people are telling. Are they spinning yarns in the pub about how their ingenuity was blocked by mindless bureaucracy? How someone they liked has been mistreated? Or, in contrast, are they retelling anecdotes about their team's amazing achievements? Or their manager's bravery in sticking up for them?

Simple stories have been told by humans to reaffirm their group identity for millennia. Somewhere along the line that got lost in a lot of businesses. As a result, many company meetings, conferences and away days could be marketed as powerful cures for insomnia. They are dominated by sterile, mindless PowerPoint-based presentations that nobody cares about or remembers. To reverse this depressing trend in your company, listen carefully for great stories that embody the culture you want to see: tales of perseverance, passion and customer service.

☀ Celebrate heroes: retell great stories that represent your culture. Don't worry about repeating yourself. We were all children once. Just like children, we like to hear a good story more than once.

Electric conclusion

Your creative climate drives the behaviour of your employees. An appropriate culture is vital and needs to be aligned with your purpose and commercial strategy. It is particularly crucial when creativity, innovation and electric conversations are not just jam, but your daily bread. So, just as the founders of the Eden Project realised the prevailing Cornish weather conditions would fail to produce lemon trees and coffee plants, we need to accept that the standard culture in most businesses will fail to produce great ideas. Something needs to be done.

The Silicon Valley media-streaming business Netflix has a cultural mantra: 'Great workplace is stunning colleagues': one person's excellence is valuable to the rest of the team. High-performing stars will help you attract and retain other stars. Develop and maintain your own unique climate filled with a buzzing static charge and the sparks of ideas by practising the approaches above – and in the rest of this book. It leads to a virtuous circle in which talent should be knocking at the front door of your biome trying to get in.

Sparks to remember

➤ Culture is 'the way things get done around here'. But a creative culture is not the same as a comfortable culture.

➤ Culture eats strategy for breakfast and drives key behaviours.

➤ To encourage a creative and collaborative climate, become a culture detective: lead by example and tell inspiring stories.

➤ You don't need to spend millions to change culture; but, if you do invest a little bit, you'll get a great return through the power of the creative business virtuous circle.

CLEAR steps to change

Communicate

Measure the spark in your culture 1: Put aside a few hours and arrange an informal meeting. Perhaps, spring for some quality coffee and breakfast. Gather together people who really know your business. They may not have been there the longest, or be the most senior. They are, in your opinion, stars; people who represent the culture at its best, or how it should be.

Ask them: how is creativity being promoted in this business? What was the last good idea each of them had, and what did they do with it? What can be done to encourage everyone in the business to reassess how things are being done, how projects are being handled and how customers are being served? Ensure you act as a non-judgemental facilitator of this session. The idea is to listen.

Learn

Measure the spark in your culture 2: Gather feedback. If it's good, bad or middling, record it all on a flip chart and boil down the main points.

Energise

Measure the spark in your culture 3: At the end of the feedback session decide what you will do with this information. Make some changes? Communicate it to a wider group? Ask some more people? The decision is yours to make. These structured discussions, and the actions that flow from them, are how creative climates get made or unmade. Here are few themes that might emerge:

■ What can you do to **remove distractions** from your most talented people? This could be as simple and cost-free as organising a discount deal at a local gym or investing in productivity-enhancing laptops or smart phones.

- What little touches could you make to the **physical environment** to encourage chance conversations, fun, and employee empowerment?
- Be creative. How can you change the physical environment to make it easier to meet, share ideas and showcase great work and stories? Send the following message:
  - We want to support you. We care about you and your environment.
  - We want work to be somewhere you enjoy being.
  - We want to bring work and fun together.
  - We want you to mix – and have electric conversations.

Act

Your changes:

- **Electric conversation**: Follow Gandhi's advice and 'Be the change you wish to see in the world': encourage creativity by sparking an electric conversation with a colleague.
- **Story-telling leader**: Find a great story that illustrates the behaviours in your ideal culture and tell it informally to the people on your team. Encourage them to tell you what they think of the story and share their own stories with you.

Environment changes:

- **Removing distractions**: Work at taking distractions away from your team until it is a more playful environment.
- **Physical environment**: Make some changes to the physical environment to make it more collaborative and inspiring.

Respond

By its nature, the leadership of an organisational culture is an ongoing neverending process. From time to time, use the exercises above to take the temperature of your business culture – then influence it with your leadership style and behaviours.

Balance focus with freedom
How to manage creative tensions

You'll learn:

- How to communicate the tensions in a creative business
- How to judge the balance between focus and freedom
- How to avoid 'rule creep'
- How to provide context rather than control
- How to use the four Ts to empower your employees to discretionary effort

"If you want to build a ship, don't drum up people to gather wood, divide the work and give orders. Instead, teach them to yearn for the vast and endless sea."
Antoine de Saint-Exupery, writer, aviator and author.

Management at the Silicon Valley media start-up Netflix was determined to treat employees like 'fully formed adults'. So, they set up an honour system for time off. Employees kept track of holidays and let their manager know when they'd be out of the office. But, when the business floated on the stock market, the appointed auditors hit the roof; insisting the business needed to implement a costly new system to account for time off 'properly'.

These bureaucratic demands contravened the Netflix phobia of 'rule creep'.[1] Feeling this was something important, CEO Reed Hastings asked chief talent officer Patty McCord to check if this request was strictly necessary under Californian law. It turned out it wasn't, so Netflix went in the opposite direction. It informed salaried employees they should take whatever time off they thought was appropriate. Hasting's reasoning was employees were already working many hours at night and at the weekend that were unaccounted. The business wasn't tracking hours worked per day, so why should it track holidays taken per year?

This remarkably trusting adult-to-adult relationship with staff is also clearly signalled in the Netflix expenses policy. Most businesses have complex rules around travel and entertaining policed by finance departments. Netflix's policy is five words long: 'Act in Netflix's best interests'. McCord writes: 'Bosses and employees were asked to work it out with one another. We did provide some guidance. If you worked in accounting or finance, you shouldn't plan to be out at the beginning or the end of the quarter, because those were the busy times. If you wanted 30 days off in a row, you needed to meet with HR.' There were also a few other commonsense principles to clarify what 'best interest' means:

- Expense only what you would otherwise not spend.
- Travel as if it were your own money.
- Take from Netflix only when it would be inefficient not to take – for example, people are free to take a reasonable number of personal phone calls at work or print off personal documents.

With these simple guidelines, Netflix is urging staff to 'grow up' – to act like they own the business: to act like self-disciplined and adult leaders. To be the sort of person who doesn't wait to be told what to do. All great creative businesses offer their people enormous freedom. It works for Netflix: as well as stunning commercial success, it won three Emmy awards in 2013.

※ **Help your staff to 'grow up'. Replace a parent-child relationship with an adult-to-adult dialogue.**

Managing creative tensions

Creative businesses are chock full of creative tensions. For anyone who craves a clear-cut, black-and-white existence it can be a challenge. Balancing day-to-day tensions and striving for seeming opposites can seem strange. An innovative company is riddled with perilous balances – it's a defining feature. It's all about embracing this reality, rather than fighting it.

Dame Gail Rebuck, chairman of the UK arm of Penguin Random House, puts it this way: 'To manage a creative business is like navigating a sea of paradoxes. Anyone who can't cope with that probably shouldn't be in a creative business. Our role is to balance the two ends of the see saw and somehow knit the paradox together. Creative people love certainty – they like to think they live in a protective microcosm. So, I always thought my role was to be a rock of certainty in this uncertain universe. To be calm … not to panic. Being a creative leader is like handing out life rafts the whole time while navigating the currents of change.'[2]

Coping with the tensions in a creative business follows the logic of a brainstorm. You defer judgement at the beginning, knowing an environment with less negative criticism will help bring out more courageous ideas. But we know at some point we'll need to pick good ideas, and kill the bad ones. Creative leaders therefore need to develop the skill to intervene at the right moment during the process, to bring in commercial reality at the right time. It sounds odd but, in the same process, they need to be non-judgemental and then, at some point, they need to be judgemental. There's no formula for this – it's based on intuition, empathy for the people coming up with the ideas and experience.

Managing director of Lion TV Nick Catliff makes for a great lunch companion. Fast and funny, he's insightful about what makes a creative business tick. He's equally committed to commercial success **and** creative excellence. He believes managing tensions is the essence of creative leadership: 'It's about being pulled in different directions. A director says to me he needs an extra day shooting, but I need him to be on budget. That tension requires a judgement call about the value of that extra day. And it's not about balance. Balance implies a calm decision-making process and that you know all the facts and can judge the outcome. You don't. You're managing tensions.'[3] Creative business leaders have to live with this Yin & Yang of creative business; here are just a few more tensions:

- Creativity versus commerciality
- Time to create versus urgency to deliver
- Supportive to staff versus challenging to staff
- Excellence versus accepting failure
- Delivering what customers want versus delivering what customers need
- Profit in proven products versus investment in unproven products
- Living the values versus challenging the status quo
- Process-focused versus goal-focused
- Serious versus fun

First, let's explore the benefits of laser-like focus. Then we'll turn 180 degrees to see why clarity always needs to be leavened with freedom.

※ Identify your creative tensions, then find the right balance between freedom and a focus for your team.

Focus

Focus at business level

"You can't depend on your eyes when your imagination is out of focus."
Mark Twain, writer

When Steve Jobs came back to Apple in 1997 it was in a mess. It was just a few months away from bankruptcy, with a dwindling 4 per cent share of the PC market and annual losses exceeding $1 billion. Three CEOs had come and gone in a decade; board members had tried to sell the company but found no takers. At the time, rival CEO Michael Dell said, if he ran Apple, he'd 'shut it down and give the money back to shareholders'.[4]

The company was selling a wide, and rather confusing, array of computers and add-ons. There were a dozen different versions of the Macintosh alone. In the first few weeks after he came back, Jobs sat through hours of review sessions about the product portfolio. Finally, he'd heard enough. 'Stop! This is crazy,' he shouted. In the stunned silence he grabbed a marker, stalked up to the whiteboard and drew a simple two-by-two grid. At the top of the two columns he wrote 'Consumer' and 'Pro'. Then he labelled the two rows 'Desktop' and 'Portable'. He turned around and made an announcement that changed the strategy and the fortunes of the business. He told his team their job was to focus on developing just four products – one for each square in the grid. He added one more thing: all other products should be cancelled.

Jobs definitively answered the crucial strategy question: Where is your focus? Put another way: What do you want to say 'yes' to? What do we want to say 'no' to? He later remarked: 'What not to do is as important as deciding what to do. That's true for companies, and it's true for products.' Focus was dear to Jobs' heart – and one of the reasons why the business became so successful after he returned to the helm.

After he'd turned the business around, he made a habit of taking the top leaders on a retreat each year. On the final day he would stand at the whiteboard and ask: 'What are the 10 things we are going to do next?' His lieutenants would fight to get their idea on the board. As the discussion subsided, 10 potential products would remain. At this point, Jobs would cross off seven explaining: 'We can only do three.'[5]

What he meant, of course, is Apple could do only three things brilliantly well and better than the competition. Jobs' almost pathological urge to focus, to pare down, to simplify has become an Apple motif. He once declared: 'Simplicity is the ultimate sophistication.' You can see this philosophy at work if you compare Apple's software with its rival, Microsoft. As Microsoft becomes ugly and complicated with added features, Apple follows a focused design ethic of simplicity.

The kid in a sweetshop

Focus should be a mantra for any business. But it is particularly important when plying your trade in new ideas. There's precious little that's tangible about a knowledge business. The only thing to see is an office, some laptops and people. Value lies in the unique culture, the creative energy and that most modern of assets: intellectual property in the form of brands, patents, copyright and trademarked processes. This lighter-than-air quality leads to agility, an entrepreneurial spirit and a flexibility that's exciting and full of potential. But there's an ever-present challenge: if you can turn your hand to pretty much anything, what do you say no to?

Creative people can do anything, and they often try. I call it the 'kid in a sweetshop' syndrome. Everything looks so appetising and interesting management ends up trying to do everything, being average at everything, and feeling a bit sick when it looks at the profits – and the success of its rivals. The key to focus is being crystal-clear about what you want to be famous for.

☀ Jot down a list of your products and services. If you were going to reduce this list by half, what would you discontinue, and why? Is anything you offer non-core and confusing for customers?

There are obvious benefits to focus on:

- **Excellence**: You get very good at what you do. Focus leads to mastery. What business professors call a 'core competence': the way your people work together. It's made of the creative attitude brought to projects, technical know-how, reliable processes and trusting relationships with customers and suppliers. Understanding what you're good at as a team or a business provides a liberating focus. For example, Sir Richard Branson knows Virgin is not just about recording music, driving trains, providing broadband or managing financial services. It's actually about offering the best customer service. This focus has led to a uniquely Virgin core competence. Ironically, for a quality that's about focus, it's allowed Virgin to be successful in a wide variety of markets.

■ **Reputation:** Being excellent naturally leads to a good name with customers and with potential employees. Creativity is by its nature somewhat subjective – so fame is the ultimate differentiator. It is why winning an Oscar (or Cannes Lions Award or Yellow Pencil, the equivalent in advertising and design industries) is so important in the creative industries. It's not just ego. Awards bestow vital credibility on the creative output of a business. That's why it's not unknown in the advertising world to have 'awards won' as a key performance indicator in a commercial strategy.

☀ Set out to win an award for creativity or innovation in the next 12 months – then shout about it from the rooftops.

Focus at project level

Focus needs to be consistent from the dizzy heights of commercial strategy to the creative business coal face: projects. In the advertising industry they call project-level focus the 'freedom of the tight brief'.[6] An advertising brief is the hallowed document agreed with the client before work starts. It throws down a gauntlet for the agency to respond to with a creative solution. Artists intuitively understand working within rigid bounds liberates creativity: they have embraced self-imposed limitations for centuries such as canvas size and poetic forms such as sonnets or haikus. Perhaps the best-judged and most simple brief of all time was provided in 1501 by the elders of a Florentine Cathedral to a 26-year-old Italian sculptor: 'Please turn this six tonne block of marble into a statue of the biblical hero David'. The specific brief didn't stop Michelangelo from producing a masterpiece of Renaissance art; it spurred him on.[7]

The insight for creative leaders: you won't cramp someone's creative style by presenting them with a focused business objective and clear criteria. In fact the opposite is true. When people understand the rules of the game, they play more creatively to arrive at an ingenious solution. On the other hand, if you want to kill creativity, start with a blurred focus or move the goalpost every few weeks.

☀ Set people free by providing a tight brief for all creative projects. People work best when they have clear boundaries within which to play.

Context, not control

It is about providing sufficient insight for people to make good decisions within their teams or projects, as shown in the following table.

Good context	Too much control
Make overall strategy and assumptions clear	Top-down decision making
Provide a tight brief	Management approval needed for new ideas or small changes in direction
Link goals to company objectives	Management by committee
Define roles and responsibilities	Planning and process valued over results
Provide transparent decision making	
Prioritise deliverables	
Communicate project success criteria	

Source: From Netflix, 'Reference guide on our freedom and responsibility culture' 2009, p.78.

Time travel

In August 1963, on the steps of the Lincoln Memorial in Washington, DC, Martin Luther King delivered his spine-tingling 'I have a dream' speech. In front of 250,000 people he poetically described a USA free of racial prejudice. It was an electric sermon built around a single phrase, 'I have a dream'. It still has the ability to move people today. When you speak from the heart, people respond.

You need to provide a focused vision of the future for your employees or team members. A vision is how the world will look and sound when your business or team succeeds in its objectives. Visions don't have to be flashes of rhetorical genius like Martin Luther King's; but they do need to inspire. It can be as simple as what your office might feel like when it changes for the better. To be a success it needs to engage employees with the excitement of joining forces to make them come true.

Once upon a time ...

I once worked with an introverted and highly intelligent MD who had been asked by a global board to turn around an under-performing operating company. I challenged him to be creative about communicating his vision for the future. It was an urgent task, as employees desperately needed some encouragement in what was a very tough time. He took the exercise to heart. A week later he emailed me with a document, which began: 'Once upon a time ...' Using the structure of a simple first-person story, he'd skilfully painted a picture of what he was seeing, hearing and feeling on a typical day in the office three years in the future. He gave it real colour, humour and emotion – talking about the team's joy when they won a particular client (which at that point was with a competitor), as well as the pride and emotion of energising a flagging culture. His management team listened in silence. They were clearly surprised to see this quiet and calm guy had such burning passion hidden away underneath his rather cool surface. After giving him an unexpected round of applause (I think they even surprised themselves), they asked him to repeat the story at an all-staff event the following week. His vision inspired many people in the business to turn things around.

☀ Step into your own time machine. Travel three years into the future. Create a vision for your team by writing a story about what you see, hear and feel. You can even draw a picture. This is a creative way to find out what inspires you personally – so you can communicate it to others.

Freedom

"Creativity is the residue of time wasted."
Albert Einstein

With focus, offer freedom. Once you have pointed out the mountain you want your people to conquer, don't be too prescriptive about how they should climb it. Point at a challenging snow-covered peak in the distance and exclaim: 'I don't care how you do it; just get to the top of that.' Non-creative businesses offer the following prescription:

- First, put on your boots.
- Second, use the handy and detailed map provided for you by your line manager.
- Third, lean your body weight forward and swing your right leg. You are now what we call 'walking'.
- Fourth...

You get the picture.

Gordon Torr, author and former creative director of JWT, one of the world's biggest advertising agencies, puts it this way: 'We should be absolutely clear what "freedom of process" means. It means: in the period between the brief and the creative solution, complete autonomy needs to be granted to the creative people involved. This includes the freedom to work on it where they want to, when they want to and how they want to. It means they must be trusted to use their time and available resources in the way that suits them, not in the way that suits the company. It means that their performance will be measured only on the quality of the result and not on the way in which they want to go about getting there.'[8] The advertising agency Ogilvy & Mather expressed it like this: 'We don't like rigid pecking orders. We give our executives an extraordinary degree of independence, in the belief that freedom stimulates initiative. We dislike issuing orders; the best results are produced by men and women who don't have to be told what to do.'[9]

Freedom to experiment

Spencer Silver is famous in the world of business innovation because he failed. In 1968 Silver was a young scientist working at the Minnesota Mining and Manufacturing Company. He was trying to develop super-strong glue, but he got it completely wrong. Instead of developing tough, muscular glue, he came up with the opposite: weedy, weakling glue that was sticky only when some pressure was applied. But, Silver was a determined young man and promoted his 'invention' within the company for five long years, despite the inevitable jibes and jokes. Things weren't great for Silver, but then serendipity struck.

In 1974, a colleague called Art Fry came up with the idea of using the glue to anchor a bookmark in his hymnbook. Because the glue was not very tacky, it was also reusable and so perfect for something that might need to be stuck to surfaces more than once. Buoyed up by his small success, Fry continued to work on applications for the glue in what the Minnesota Mining and Manufacturing Company called 'bootlegging time': hours put aside for scientists to run free and develop their own ideas.

Offering this freedom in the 1960s must have seemed like a big risk. But it paid off. The company now offers more than 600 products using the weedy glue in more than 100 countries.[10] When you look down at your desk you'll probably catch sight of the result of Spencer's failure, and Art's perseverance: the humble Post-It Note. Now an established office icon, the Post-It Note is not so humble in terms of profit. The Minnesota Mining and Manufacturing Company has now shortened its rather unwieldy name to 3M. It makes and sells more than 55,000 products worldwide: everything from waterproof sandpaper to Scotchlite, the reflective material that helps people to be more visible on roads at night. The business is now ranked as the third-most innovative company in the world.[11] Its culture of invention is reflected in an impressive statistic: 30 per cent of its $30 billion sales come from new products.[12]

Bootlegging time is now called 15 per cent time in 3M: how long every week 3M people spend pursuing speculative ideas that are not necessarily anything to do with their job specification. 3M is famous for pioneering the peculiar idea that workers should do as they please for some of the time. You can see why: big breakthroughs come when people venture beyond their area of expertise and start asking dumb questions like 'Why don't we try it this way instead?' As with all speculative, creative endeavours this leads to a lot of 'wasted time'. But it also produces the occasional acorn – like the Post-It Note – that grows to be a mighty oak.

Enlightened companies have picked up on this idea of offering autonomy for new product development:

- Google upped the stakes and increased the free time for its people to a day a week – 20 per cent time. It asks its engineers to choose what takes their fancy – from fixing an existing product to something entirely new. Google News, Gmail, Google Talk, Google Sky and Google Translate have all come from this ability to work autonomously.[13] Google says its most successful innovations are the ones that bubble up from the ranks.[14]

- Corning makes the tough Gorilla Glass that graces the front of iPhones.[15] Its R&D lab requires scientists to spend 10 per cent of their time on 'Friday afternoon experiments' to develop 'slightly crazy ideas'. Sometimes they are pet 'passion' projects superiors have discontinued. For instance, a Corning genomics technology business was developed on an idea that was officially killed by the head of research – but doggedly pursued on Friday afternoons.[16]

- Swiss pharmaceutical company Novartis encourages scientists to spend a portion of their time working on drugs for 'niche' diseases. The criteria consists of two questions: 1) Is it scientifically possible to develop?; and 2) Does it meet an unmet medical need? Note they don't ask the question 'What's the market?'; but instead, 'Is there a patient suffering who could be cured with today's knowledge?'[17]

- Linden Lab, the company that manages the virtual world, Second Life, claims the autonomy offered to workers leads to the company's greatest success stories.[18]

- Every quarter, Australian software company Atlassian encourages its 400 or so 'geeks, beer drinkers, nerf herders, fraggers, and Wolverine-wannabes' to participate in '24-hour hackathons'. They were originally called 'Fedex Days' because employees deliver the project overnight.[19]

These managerial decisions are supported by comprehensive analysis of creative success. A study of patents filed by 11,000 research and development employees found workers were more fired up by their work – and filed more patents – when projects were intellectually challenging and **independently motivated**. Self-motivated employees filed many more patents than those solely motivated by salary, benefits and job security.[20]

☀ Encourage your people to innovate upon products and services which they actually want to use. This passionate engagement delivers a powerful electric jolt of motivation a salary just can't match.

The four Ts

Offering freedom can seem daunting and, of course, it does involve some risk. So it helps to break it into the four Ts, listed below. In this way you can decide in which areas, and how far you want to go:[21]

- **Time:** Could you introduce your own version of bootlegging time? If this sounds a bit radical, could you trial it as a single workshop, or an away day to see what comes out? What criteria are you going to use for what the project should be about? 100 per cent freestyle? Improving 'something annoying' in the way you do things now?

- **Task:** Developing a system in which it is possible for people to put themselves forward for the projects that excites them. Matching people with the right projects at the right time is the key to great people management.

■ Team: Allowing people to lobby to move on to different teams, or poach talent from elsewhere in the business for their team. Allow supply and demand for talent to help you reward your most effective and creative people.

■ Technique: Offering people the widest possible latitude to the 'how?' of their job. Can you introduce some feedback in your processes to find out if the people on the front line might find a better way? The old-fashioned suggestion box is only a laughing stock because so many companies have failed to put good ideas into practice.

☀ Take the risk out of offering autonomy to staff by using the 4 Ts – Time, Task, Team and Technique – to offer freedom little-by-little.

Ignore the boss

The production of a film shares a lot of characteristics with a business project. A key cast and technical crew are brought together at the right time during the project to produce something that's never been seen before. The director's role is to guide the creative process to achieve his or her vision. It is a potent analogy for creative tension: a balance between following direction and the possibility for individual acts of artistic and technical creativity by actors, cinematographers, animators and editors.

Legendary director Woody Allen is unusual. He invents most of the central ideas for his films himself, as well as writing the script. You would think this would make him obsessively controlling of his vision; quite the reverse. In fact, Allen has been called 'the least directing of directors'. Over five decades of making films, he's honed a simple way of getting the best out of creative people:

1 Hire the best talent you can find.

2 Allow them as much freedom as possible.

3 Ask their opinion of how things should be done.

In 1995 a young actress, Mira Sorvino, landed a central role as a prostitute and part-time porn star in Woody Allen's film *Mighty*

Aphrodite. Naturally, she expected to be told what to do by the great man. So, she was taken aback when he turned to her and said: 'You don't have to say any of the words I've written, if you don't want to.' She recounted: 'I was shocked. Because I was like: This is the best genius comedy writer we have; his script is so fantastic, why wouldn't I say the words?' But Allen insisted, telling her: 'The script is just a blueprint. It's whatever makes you as funny and natural as possible; so, if you want to say something else, go ahead and say it.' Mira followed his advice and won an Academy Award for the role.

Woody Allen has a very clear vision for all of his film projects. But he knows it will be more vibrant and interesting if his co-collaborators bring their ideas to the party. His allowance for deviation from the blueprint has its limits. The actors must stick to the intention of the scene and the lines they are ad libbing around. But, if they comply with this, they can then make the part their own. It means they are keen to give their very best. The actor Josh Brolin, who starred in Allen's 2010 film *You Will Meet a Tall Dark Stranger*, puts it simply: 'He's just one of these guys you want to please.' The paradoxical outcome of a leader's confidence in allowing freedom is summed up by Larry David, the writer of *Seinfeld* and *Curb Your Enthusiasm*, who has appeared in Allen's films: 'This notion I hear that he doesn't direct is kind of ridiculous. He gets what he wants.'[22]

The co-founder of Hewlett Packard, David Packard, brags in his book, *The HP Way*, about an employee who took this idea of freedom so far he disobeyed a direct order. Chuck House was working at HP's lab in Colorado Springs, devoted to oscilloscope technology. He was told in no uncertain terms to abandon the development of a display monitor. He ignored his supervisor and embarked on a holiday to California – taking his own time to stop along the way to show potential customers the prototype. He even persuaded his R&D manager to rush the monitor into production. Some years later, at a gathering of HP engineers, Packard presented Chuck with a medal for 'extraordinary contempt and defiance beyond the normal call of engineering duty'. The monitor resulted in sales of $35 million.

☀ Encourage employees to ignore the boss from time to time. Offering freedom means allowing employees to 'pull rank' to support a good idea.

Box ticking versus going the extra mile

In 2013 Swindon Borough Council in the south of England asked contractors to paint double yellow lines in the alleyways behind some houses to prevent parked cars blocking the way. They gave detailed instructions. Most of the job was done satisfactorily. The reason the story achieved national media attention was the instructions failed to mention the contractors were not supposed to paint lines in the narrow pedestrian alleyways next to the roads. The result: a number of alleyways efficiently painted with yellow lines on each side with a gap between them of 33cm – about the width of a laptop. A local commented with admirable understatement it was a 'bit of a mystery' as 'you couldn't even fit a motorbike down it'.

Telling people exactly what to do all the time is a dangerous game in any business. The world is more complicated than any rule-book you can write. A rules-based, box-ticking culture steals away any impulse for independent thought. It might buy compliance, but at a heavy cost. The opposite happens when an employee is so inspired by creative business values that they go the extra mile. While working with Virgin Media I stumbled upon a powerful example. A call centre operative was scanning the records of her team when she came across multiple complaints from Graham, a particularly tricky customer.[23] He'd been phoning day-in day-out, saying he couldn't work the remote control for Virgin Media's set-top box. He wasn't happy; the problem hadn't been resolved. The Virgin employee knew calling him back would take time. But she did it anyway. After genuinely listening, she did something remarkable. She found a remote control for the box in question and took it home. She rooted around in her garage, found a spray can, removed the remote's facia, painted it white, replaced it, and posted the customised remote to the customer. The next day she received an email enthusiastically thanking her. He was partially sighted so he hadn't been able to make out the remote's black buttons against the standard black facia. Amongst the Virgin values, written on the wall near the employee's desk, are three she delivered on with one small act of kindness: *insatiable curiosity, heartfelt service* and *delightfully surprising*. Virgin Media is now developing a range of different colours for all its remote controls.

☀ **Work with human nature, not against it. Allow people freedom to approach work in their own unique, creative way. People are more knowledgeable about projects they develop from their own passions and interests.**

Electric conclusion

Managing a company for new ideas is paradoxical; resolving creative tensions goes with the territory. Leaders and managers need to ensure everyone in the business is aware of the balance required between focus and freedom.

Of course, freedom is not absolute. It's like free speech. Just as it's illegal to shout 'Fire!' in a theatre, it should be against the rules to do anything that might be dangerous or unethical in a business. And there are some markets – such as nuclear power, medicine and health and safety – where freedom clearly needs to be more tightly subscribed. But the empowering philosophy of focus **and** freedom works for all managers seeking to increase creativity. Point to a mountain, but let employees decide their route to the top.

Sparks to remember

➤ Creative businesses are a balance between focus and freedom – and other creative tensions.

➤ Focus should be a mantra for a creative business because it produces excellence and fame.

➤ You won't cramp creativity by presenting employees with a focused business brief; understanding the rules of the game means you are more creative, not less.

➤ There needs to be focus for commercial strategy and projects.

➤ As leader you need to provide a forward-looking focus: an inspiring vision of the future.

➤ As a manager offer context, not control – and as much freedom as possible.

➤ Don't forget: creative freedom is an invitation for employees to ignore the boss from time to time.

CLEAR steps to change

Communicate

Bring up the idea of how a business manages creative tensions in your next team meeting.

Learn

Ask your team's opinion how well this tricky balance is being struck right now. Listen carefully to their feedback before engaging in an open dialogue about how the team can improve or change.

Energise

■ **Focus cascade**: Focus from top to bottom. Design an organisational system whereby your business' and team's strategic objectives are linked to tactical team goals. And then encourage everyone to develop personal performance goals to support the team and the organisation.

- **Four Ts freedom**: Look for small and large ways to empower people in how they choose their approach to **time** spent at work, the **task** they work on, the **team** they work with and the **technique** they use. Be careful not to overwhelm less experienced staff members: freedom can be scary.

Act

- **Focus**: Play the 'What's our value proposition?' game with your management team. List your products on one side of a whiteboard, and your competitors on the other. In the middle, brainstorm which competitors duplicate, or even outperform, your offering to the market. What's left? Think about dropping the 'me-too' products and focusing on your genuine value proposition.

- **Freedom**: Experiment! Put some free time aside for people to pursue passion projects. Don't necessarily make it a regular thing straight away; find the best way it works for you.

Respond

Six months from now, look to see how your team's behaviours have changed with more focus *and* more freedom. Is the balance right?

Demolish idea barriers
How to dynamite the walls that block creativity

You'll learn:

- How to identify and demolish organisational barriers to good ideas
- How to avoid killing creativity as you grow
- How to develop an outward-facing collaborative culture

"The barriers are not erected which can say to aspiring talents and industry, 'Thus far and no farther.'"
Ludwig van Beethoven, composer

Channel 4 is an advertiser-funded broadcaster founded by British government charter. The charter decrees Channel 4 has to deliver innovative content to the UK. This unique legal status means external collaboration is not just a good idea – it's mandatory. Be creative, or break the law. In fact, Channel 4 doesn't make any programmes. The business commissions all its creative content from a pool of around 500 external suppliers ranging from one-man band start-ups to global TV producers.[1]

To ensure geographic diversity, Channel 4 is required to source about a third of its programmes from outside London and from the smaller nations of the UK – Scotland, Wales and Northern

Ireland. On top of these legal rules, voluntary management policies ensure restless change: job descriptions for commissioners make it clear they have to work with a certain number of new businesses every year. Being a 'publisher-broadcaster' has proved to be an advantage. Channel 4 can spot promising ideas, wherever they come from. For example, the reality TV show *Big Brother* was picked up from a Dutch company, Endemol, and developed by Channel 4 into a money-spinning UK hit. 'Working with different suppliers is a big part of our success,' explains director of creative diversity Stuart Cosgrove in his gravelly Scottish accent. 'It means we can navigate change more effectively. We haven't built up big, inflexible in-house production functions. If we want to change the nature of what we do, we don't have a department we have to make redundant. We just shift the radar of our creative commissioning.'

Channel 4 knows it must be careful not to become too reactive and dependent on others for the creative spark. 'As well as being a strength, there is an inherent danger in the outsourcing model,' Cosgrove explains. 'We know we must avoid waiting for creativity to drop into our in-box.' To proactively set the agenda for suppliers, Channel 4 executives invest two hours every week in a freewheeling discussion of the next big thing. The output of this get-together provides a tight brief for external producers. 'In higher education you'd probably call it a seminar!' laughs Cosgrove. 'Over breakfast every week we have a wide-ranging chat. Today it was about the topic of the pros and cons of London as a Super City. We don't necessarily get to a finished idea. We're looking to see tram lines of change. Sometimes the meeting leads to a dead end. But sometimes it leads to a commission, some new research, or the pursuit of a new avenue.'

Cosgrove argues the core of the channel's creative success is derived from a 'culture of curiosity'. It's propagated from the moment a new person is inducted. Staff feedback shows employees are very proud of the business' purpose. Cosgrove added: 'If you are not engaged with the core innovative purpose of this organisation, it's highly unlikely you will survive here very long. But we don't insist people sign up like it's some kind of religion;

that might squash their curiosity or lead to a fear of failure.' To ensure people 'fit in' the business takes great pains to find and hire focused, ambitious talent who have been innovative before coming into Channel 4. 'We have to ensure the people that are in creative dialogue with the best suppliers, are themselves the best in the business,' argues Cosgrove.

Cosgrove's creative diversity team is an investment to ensure Channel 4 takes risks. He explains: 'I have two metaphors for what we do. We are like the music industry A&R [artists and repertoire] men, looking for the next hit band. But we are also Sherpas: we understand how to navigate the "Channel 4 Mountain". So, we help external suppliers to work the system, get quality meetings and improve their own creativity.' The team also distributes a £2 million seed fund each year to outside businesses in small chunks of £5–10,000. The Alpha Fund is earmarked for developing promising new ideas. Cosgrove estimates only 20 per cent of the shows funded by Alpha money get commissioned; and under 10 per cent then go on to be hits. 'But you can dine out on those for years,' he laughs.[2]

☀ Organise your own blue skies meeting about the 'Next Big Thing'. No agenda. Invite people to come along with customer stories, snippets from magazines, YouTube videos and new ideas – anything to give the discussion a creative spark.

Clear out the cobwebs

When businesses start up, they are always creative. But, as they grow up, they seem to lose that energetic, entrepreneurial spirit. What happens? Dame Gail Rebuck, chairman of the UK arm of Penguin Random House, says she is always shocked by the latticework of bureaucracy that grows over time. 'You have to constantly go back into the attic and clear out the cobwebs,' she said. 'Rules put in place to solve a particular problem linger on long after the person who put it in has forgotten about it because the problem's moved on. Old initiatives that were important at the time then clog up the system.'[3]

☀ Spring clean old rules that are no longer relevant.

Businesses walk through stable periods of evolution until it becomes obvious the way it is organised doesn't match the changed world it now inhabits. It then hits a crisis.[4] When you've worked with lots of businesses, as I have, you realise these crises are actually predictable, necessary and valuable. A better name for them is turning points: they present an opportunity for the business to grow up. How often these crises occur depends on the rate of business growth and industry change. But the managerial response to them can erect bureaucratic barriers that stifle creativity later on. Here are three common crises – and the barriers erected as a result – that I've observed over the years:

1 **Leadership Crisis**: An entrepreneurial business is growing fast through creativity and good ideas. But one day they realise chaotic day-to-day creativity is not enough. The management team decides: 'We need a clear direction!' Professional management and planning is introduced. But, if it's not handled well, there is trouble in store. Result: too much directive management stifles initiative.

2 **Middle Management Crisis**: The business gets even bigger. It becomes clear: 'We need more mid-level managers!' New structures are introduced, based on delegation. But, this is done without sufficient people development. Result: middle managers don't understand the values and behaviour required to run a creative business.

3 **Control Crisis**: The business expands further – perhaps branching out overseas. Middle management can't cope with the level of complexity and demands on its time. The board decides: 'We're out of control!' The response is to create separate departments, as well as support functions like finance, HR and marketing. But, the new system is not supported by improved communication. Result: the business is too bureaucratic and fails to promote sufficient collaboration.

☀ **Think about the growth crises your business has gone through. Identify any of the managerial responses they provoked that are now crushing creativity – and get rid of them.**

Of course, all businesses need to professionalise and go through these rights of passage in one way or another. Bureaucracy is not a dirty word – it can be necessary and sensible. If businesses can't change, they end up in crisis mode perpetually. As a business grows, there will be a tendency to respond to predictable crises by building hierarchy, specialised roles, permanent departments and a more formal structure. If you are not careful, people stop communicating. You build internal and external barriers, which kill collaboration. Like humans, companies tend to base their habits on previous events and experiences. This leads to organisations fully equipped to deal with the past; but less and less equipped to deal with the future.

Superficially, it seems like there are three unattractive options for growth:[5]

1 Stay creative by staying small.
2 Try to avoid rules as you grow (which leads to chaos).
3 Develop complex rules and processes as you grow to drive efficient execution but cripple creativity and the ability to respond to change as a result.

Of course, the best option is to grow the business in a way that actively encourages collaboration: and become **more** creative as you get bigger. That's what this habit (and the next) is all about. It's your job to become aware of barriers and occasionally dynamite these walls to preserve and nurture the rampant creativity of the company's younger, wilder days. There are six barriers you need to be particularly aware of: size, silos, lack of serendipity, lack of serious talent, supreme leaders and not-invented-here syndrome, as shown in Figure 9.1.

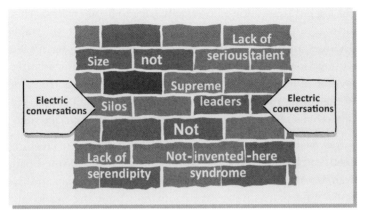

figure 9.1 Idea barriers

1 Size

The entrepreneurs I work with are always dreading the moment when their company loses its mojo. They fear at a certain size the business will become bureaucratic, leaden and uncreative. Meanwhile, the executives I work with in bigger, global businesses often bemoan the red tape that encircles them. Intuitively we know it's a little easier to communicate, collaborate and be creative in a smaller business. After all, if you're all in one room, it's less effort to share information and nimbly relocate people from one project to another. Jonah Lehrer, in his research on how imagination works in business, describes how large companies lose the plot: 'They keep people from relaxing and having insights. They stifle conversations, discourage dissent, and suffocate social networks. Rather than maximising employee creativity, they become obsessed with minor inefficiencies.'[6] A remarkable survey of more than 8,500 publicly traded companies in the USA showed, as the number of employees grew, profit per employee **shrank**.[7] This shouldn't happen. It defies the basic economic logic of economies of scale (as you get bigger you can do things more cheaply). For creativity, size clearly matters.

But big businesses don't necessarily have to be uncreative. They have a lot going for them: strong client relationships, stable finances and the ability to take the kind of long-term view required for leading a creative culture. So, why do they so often become unimaginative? The researchers in the study above came to the conclusion the businesses in question failed to reap the expected benefits of size because of their inability to collaborate.

A way to encourage collaboration – and to fight the creeping death of turning into a 'big, stupid' business – is to stay small, even as you get bigger. A study spanning Europe, Japan and the USA found many innovative companies limit the headcount of their operating units to fewer than 400 employees. W.L. Gore & Associates is one of them. Gore is a technology business specialising in product innovation: from medical devices that treat aneurysms to high-performance GORE-TEX® fabrics. Gore has grown from a garage start-up into a 9,000-person company with sales of $3.2 billion. Management has tried to keep collaborative teamwork alive by erecting a new building in the Delaware countryside every time a team exceeds 150 people.

You can see this 'small-is-better' attitude in marketing services giants like WPP, Publicis and Omnicom. These are global service businesses that have become dominant by voraciously buying smaller agencies. But they don't rebrand new acquisitions to become part of a corporate whole. Instead, they encourage them to retain their identity. WPP head office plays an across-the-group role in property management, procurement, IT and knowledge sharing – but that's about it. WPP has an army of 170,000 employees, but these people don't identify with WPP. They identify with the hundreds of differently branded agencies that employ them.[8]

The 'right' group size for successful collaboration might be programmed into us from an earlier age. Evolutionary experts argue a human tribe of around 150 is bred into our DNA because this is how many people banded together in pre-historic clans.[9] So, occasionally, you may need to preserve barriers around smaller collaborative groups within a larger business. But, even if a business chooses to keep operating units at a certain headcount there still needs to be collaboration and knowledge sharing **between** these units. To ensure that happens you need to avoid silos.

2 Silos

Size is not the problem that stops electric conversations: it is attitude. A common complaint I hear when I talk to leaders is: 'We've developed a silo-mentality':

- In 2010, a former Microsoft executive revealed the giant software company developed a viable tablet computer years before Apple scored a commercial smash hit with its own model. The idea had been killed by feuding Microsoft divisions and the promising prototype had been allowed to gather dust in some gloomy basement.[10]

- Over a convivial pasta lunch in South Kensington, managing director of Lion TV Nick Catliff told me his ideas team had a name for broadcasters that had destroyed their own creative culture through silos: 'Dead Stars: when it becomes corporate, fear-driven, too marketing focused – they die. There's no inspiration. When you talk to people in Dead Stars, you know what they talk about? They don't talk about ideas – they talk about each other. They talk about who has power and who doesn't. They're terrified of passing a new idea up the chain in case their boss doesn't like it.'

☀ Review incentives – are they encouraging people to work exclusively within their own group?

Silos range from different teams hoarding information to the corrosive mistrust sown by politicking and turf wars. You don't need to be big to build silos. I've seen silos in 20-person businesses all working in the same room. When organisational barriers go up it destroys trust, fosters complacency and leads to missed opportunities.

☀ Show commitment to silo destruction by explaining the importance of collaboration. Follow up with practical measures such as networking and recruiting people from outside the silo.

3 Lack of serendipity

The physical environment can prevent serendipitous electric conversations that create the spark of ideas. Despite being a guru of the digital world, Steve Jobs knew the value of face-to-face meetings. He argued: 'There's a temptation in our networked age to think that ideas can be developed by email. That's crazy. Creativity comes from spontaneous meetings, from random discussions. You run into someone, you ask what they're doing, you say "Wow!", and soon you're cooking up all sorts of ideas.'

As a founder of Pixar he designed the HQ to make sure people bump into each other.[11] 'If you don't do that, you'll lose a lot of innovation and the magic that's sparked by serendipity. So we designed the building to make people get out of their office and mingle in the central atrium with people they may not otherwise see,' he said. At Pixar you have to visit the atrium as it acts as a hub for the front doors, the main stairs, all of the corridors, the café and mailboxes. Even the conference rooms have windows that look out onto the atrium. And, when you've finished viewing a film in the 600-seat theatre, where does the exit take you? You guessed it: the atrium. Pixar chief operating officer John Lasseter, the man behind films like *Toy Story*, *Cars* and *A Bug's Life*, said: 'Steve's theory worked from day one. I kept running into people I hadn't seen for months. I've never seen a building that promoted collaboration and creativity as well as this one.' Other businesses have followed suit:

- In 2012, the London-based advertising agency Bartle Bogle Hegarty (BBH) took the decision to redesign its Central London office to make it a more playful, collaborative creative space. Executive creative director Nick Gill opened up the agency's central atrium to encourage the collision of ideas and people. It's an exciting place to visit with a central free coffee stall amid sculptures of BBH's iconic sheep dotted around the light pine floors. Creative hubs are located in positions staff are bound to walk past. These are essentially open-ended meeting rooms without walls to discuss projects and ideas. Gill said: 'It's true that your environment affects how you feel and how you work. Well, it has never felt better coming to work as it does now.'[12]

■ When BMW built its factory in Leipzig in 2005 it wanted to encourage collisions. Slightly ironic for a car maker. The facility has an open-plan layout to encourage workers to strike up spontaneous conversations and share ideas across the business.[13]

As virtual working makes tools like Skype, online networking and conferencing more sophisticated, the need for face-to-face inter-action to provoke creativity may lessen slightly. But only slightly. There will always be a need for some collaboration to take place in the same room, face-to-face.

☀ Most offices don't have an atrium. Create 'serendipitous' opportunities for staff to catch up and exchange ideas through informal off-the-cuff outings and meetings.

4 Lack of serious talent

Many companies curtail freedom as they grow, to avoid errors. It's hard to find anybody who would argue against reducing errors. But shackling employees and increasing rules, complexity and red tape has the unfortunate side effect of driving the most creative people out of the business – and into the arms of a more enlight-ened competitor. This is bearable in the short-term because fewer mistakes are made and the business is productive. However, the true cost of a brain drain reveals itself when your market changes, due to a new technology or competitive product. At this point, there is nobody left in the business with a sufficiently innovative mindset to help you respond and survive. Game over.

Netflix has a simple move to avoid disaster. Management at the US on-demand internet media business avoids 'rule creep' and 'barnacles' – its word for unnecessary products – like the plague. It argues if you focus your products and services, all you need to do is 'increase talent density faster than complexity grows'. It's a great formula for a creative business: a simple and compelling USP to retain a higher proportion of talented people in the workforce than competitors. Chief talent director Patty McCord writes: 'Our model is to increase employee freedom as we grow, rather than limit it, to continue to attract and nourish innovative people, so we have a better chance of long-term success.'[14]

5 Supreme leaders

Who's got power, and who hasn't, infuses conversations and interactions between humans. The normal leadership and management model looks like this: big bosses tell middle-size bosses what to do and they then tell everyone else (see Figure 9.2).

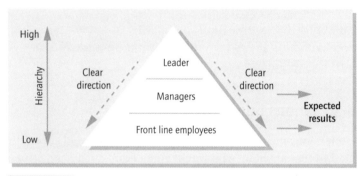

figure 9.2   The normal management model

For creative leaders the world is upside down. As much as possible, they flatten hierarchy to allow ideas to be judged objectively. They see the world in a different way from 'normal' leaders:

- Attitude: Being as available as is practical for conversations with employees – and effectively communicating the other way.
- Structure: Examining the structure of teams and departments to ensure there aren't unnecessary 'layers' of intervening

managers between the most senior person and the most junior, which block communication and slow decision making.

The oil that makes the engine run is a constant, creative and challenging electric conversation; far more likely to happen in a non-hierarchical organisation. The relationships look more like those shown in Figure 9.3.

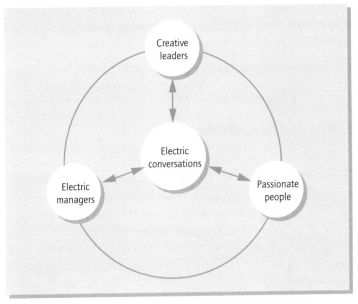

figure 9.3 **Electric conversations management model**

Here 'the work' – creativity, innovation and results – is the dominant force in the business. Everyone from leaders to freelancers is focused on ideas – rather than their place in the pecking order. Of course, creative businesses still have organisation charts. There is always a need for focus, as well as freedom. But the fundamental hierarchical assumption that the 'boss knows best' is challenged by the values of a creative business.

Liz Darran, director of brand and creative at Sky, is a great believer in removing barriers to encourage what she calls 'casual conversations'. She said: 'Encouraging creativity is about shattering hierarchy, pulling out unnecessary processes and reducing the management of complexity. You need to find the simplest possible ways for ideas to come to fruition: the least number of people in the chain. It's about building a more communicative group.' Like many other creative leaders I've worked with, Darran accepts collaboration is not always easy: 'We need to have some heat and fire in the discussions. It can't be about everyone just agreeing. You need some conflict as well as some agreement – collaboration can be both of those things. There can be friction; it doesn't need to be entirely positive.'[15]

☀ Be humble and try to keep a check on your ego: 'forget' your hierarchical position as often as you can.

5 Not-invented-here syndrome

Creative businesses avoid not-invented-here syndrome. They sidestep the self-deluded self image that arises after a modicum of success, 'nobody's as good as we are'. Sometimes the barriers that need to be demolished are between you and the rest of the world. US academic Keith Sawyer has studied collaboration in jazz bands, improvised comedy troupes, as well as commercial teams. He argues businesses need to: 'lead collaborative webs extending beyond their company's boundaries.' A top designer once winked at me and said: 'We borrow with pride!' He was referring to a willingness to listen equally to freelancers, suppliers, customers and competitors. Anyone with a good idea is worth listening to.

☀ Never stop an electric conversation at the border and ask to see its passport. Collaborate with the best you can find. No company has a monopoly on good ideas.

Collaborating with customers

Creative businesses spark electric conversations with customers while clearly communicating the opportunities and risks of innovation. Jeremy Shaw, chief operating officer of the London agency Kitcatt Nohr Digitas said: 'You have to encourage clients to trust you, and to be brave. You have to have a proper relationship with them so they can challenge what you are doing – but you can also push back. One client once said to me "Your job is to make us uncomfortable"[16]. Forming a non-hierarchical relationship with people who are signing the cheques requires a degree of honesty and self-confidence. Wally Olins, who co-founded the branding agency Wolf Olins said: 'Creative businesses need to work with clients on what they truly need. The clients and consultants need to be honest with each other. They need to co-create the brief.'[17]

Customers have always contributed to new product development. During the First World War the shortage of cotton meant army surgeons had to resort to using an absorbent substance made from wood pulp called Cellucotton. At the end of the conflict, the manufacturer Kimberly-Clark was left with a mountain of the material. But then something unexpected happened. Kimberly-Clark found that men were using Cellucotton to blow their nose. It took a while for the business to catch on, but eventually they marketed the product as a handkerchief and Kleenex blew us all away.

The digital revolution means collaboration with customers is here to stay. 'Lead users' are gold dust and companies all over the world are making the most of them:

- Lego has developed its products far beyond its simple starting point, with the aid of willing (and fairly obsessive!) customers who will play, and experiment, for free.

- Some games publishers allow 'modding' in which innovative gamers programme new features to products after they have been released.

- Amazon and eBay have based their business model on sharing a percentage of sales with an eco-system of customers and secondary sellers.

- In the hi-tech world of scientific instruments, customers are the source of over 80 per cent of all innovation.[18]

- Software business SAS has always invited customers to give feedback on their products through global forums and conferences.

- After years of holding internal 'ideas jams' with its employees, in 2006 IBM had the bright idea to invite in its customers, too.

※ Collaborate with your customers. Smart ways to get them involved with product development include focus groups, mini-conferences and online feedback.

Learning from competitors

Some businesses embark on a learning journey to embrace a new way of perceiving the competitive landscape. Facing an unprecedented wave of digital change in all of its global TV, music and book publishing concerns, the German media giant Bertelsmann knew it needed to radically change attitudes inside the business. In November 2013, it dispatched 180 of its most senior executives to 'Digital Book Camps' to learn about the disruptive trends – and the threats and opportunities – they presented. This was a significant investment; these were key decision-makers from the European TV and radio business RTL Group, global publisher Penguin Random House, Gruner + Jahr in magazines and BMG music.

But this was just the start. After achieving a consistent level of digital knowledge within the group, Bertelsmann asked them to pack their suitcases again and leave for what's recognised as the most innovative place on Earth: Silicon Valley. The leaders were treated to a week of inspirational speakers, experiences and company visits. This was a huge investment of time and money, even for a company the size of Bertelsmann, but many felt it was worth it. 'It was a life-transforming experience. I understood the trends before that, but I wasn't sure I "got it". After this I got it! It works because, if you put a creative person in a new environment, they are hardwired to learn and to change,' said Dame Gail Rebuck, UK chairman of Penguin Random House, one of the executives on the trip.

You don't need to fly your people to Silicon Valley. The creative director of a digital agency in London I know bought membership of Tate Modern for his creative team. He insisted they go to think about tough projects in the members' room, which has a stunning view of St Paul's across the Thames – as well as six floors of modern art a few minutes' away. 'It's a wonderful way to let creatives liberate their minds,' he explained.[19]

※ Get your people out of the office to learn – especially when they're stuck on a big project. Make sure they visit places and people which will challenge their preconceptions.

Open innovation

Open innovation is the idea businesses, even big ones, need to look outside if they are going to stay relevant in today's fast-changing world. In 2003, consulting firm Accenture analysed where ideas came from in 40 global companies across 5 industries. The result was striking: 45 per cent of innovation came from **outside** the business. This trend has spawned a mini-industry of online 'idea marketplaces'. These forums match experts from a variety of fields with problems that need to be solved:

- Created by the consumer products giant Procter & Gamble, Nine Sigma links scientists to knotty technical challenges.
- Founded by the global pharmaceutical company Eli Lilly, InnoCentive pays researchers financial rewards for useful solutions to difficult problems.

Nestlé invests heavily in new idea generation: spending nearly 2 per cent of revenue every year on research and development. This adds up when sales are worth €80 billion. For the last two decades, new product development has been the core of Nestlé's vision: being the world leader in 'nutrition, health and wellness'. The company employs 5,000 people in 24 internal R&D centres scattered across the world.[20] You might think this was enough. You'd be wrong. Nestlé taps into the expertise of more than a million external researchers worldwide: university and government scientists, venture capitalists and suppliers. Paul Bulcke, Nestlé's chief executive, commented: 'The biggest danger we face is that we become complacent.'[21]

Occasionally, this massive investment pays off. Take Nespresso: 'coffee-shop-quality coffee at home'. You buy a system. First, a mini version of the Starbucks-style machine, and then, each month you purchase online supplies of vacuum-packed fresh coffee capsules. It's an invention that powered the early-morning writing of this book. More importantly, it's now a €1 billion brand growing at over 40 per cent per annum.[22] The global superpower in open innovation is Procter & Gamble (P&G). P&G replaced an old-fashioned internal innovation mentality with an outward focus it calls 'connect and develop'. The results are impressive. Over a third of P&G's products are now invented in partnership with someone else. A good example is the Swiffer Duster. At the time, P&G had more PhDs on their staff than the combined university faculties of MIT, UC-Berkley and Harvard. Yet they were still struggling to come up with a new way to innovate upon the humble mop. They decided to improve their chances by working with Continuum, a specialist innovation consultancy. P&G's approach had been to tinker with chemical molecules to make a stronger cleaning fluid. Continuum tried something else: spending time with customers. A lot of time. They shot hundreds of hours of video footage in the process. One extract showed an elderly woman improvising: using a damp piece of kitchen roll on the end of a mop to pick up spilt coffee granules and then throwing the kitchen roll away. This lead to P&G's 'aha!' moment: a fabric throwaway element at the end of the mop. The Swiffer was born. The product has cleaned up (apologies), generating more than $500 million dollars in sales.[23]

⁑ Refuse to be insular and inward-looking – look outside for ideas. Partner with a university department that studies your professional discipline, find an online business forum that allows you to post and share interesting questions – or collaborate with another firm in a related field.

The CEO of a global media production business turned to me on the first morning of a major leadership development programme and whispered: 'I want this to be a particle accelerator for ideas'. We had brought together a group of executives who previously had little contact with each other. The CEO hoped the relaxed discussions and networking of a leadership programme would bring her top people together, so their ideas could collide like atoms at the speed of light. Luckily it worked just as she hoped.

Creative business people tend to be skilled and relentless networkers. Not just because they enjoy free food and drink. It's how ideas happen. Online networking helps, but a creative business thrives on the sparks created by face-to-face meetings. A defining attribute of a creative business is the importance of relationships: you need to meet with someone to get the human dynamic just right. In the advertising world 'chemistry meetings' are par for the course. It's in these encounters that electric conversations happen, half-formed ideas collide, unplanned aha! insights occur.[24]

There is growing scientific evidence proving networking grows your bottom line. Sociologists found that human beings are remarkably similar in the number of strong relationships they have in their lives. These 'strong ties' normally number between four and seven close friends. These are the people you see on a regular basis. The people you call if your house is burgled. But when it comes to 'weak ties' – people you know, but not that well – there is no such uniformity. Some of us have a handful; others have literally thousands. Take Yossi Vardi, the legendary Israeli entrepreneur and dotcom fixer. He puts people, ideas and investment together and has been an instrumental figure in the remarkable blossoming of the Israeli technology sector over the last two decades. Google co-founder Sergey Brin once said: 'If there is an internet bubble in Israel, then Vardi is the bubble.' Vardi is a world-class networker with a vast number of weak ties.

Science backs the common sense of Vardi's endless networking. For example, entrepreneurs that meet with an almost random kaleidoscope of people are three times more likely to file a patent than their colleagues with a small network. The logic is simple: your close friends have a similar set of ideas and knowledge to you: 'they know what you know'. Weak ties are far more likely to possess a new idea, left field opinion, an interesting fact that can spark creativity.[25]

But you have to work at it. Human beings are hardwired to stick to their own. Sociologists call it the 'self-similarity principle'.

That's why, when you're at a party, you end up gossiping with the person who shared a school, university or career path with you. You'll have a good time discussing common knowledge, but the conversation probably won't help you have a radical new idea.

※ Connect yourself – and your staff – to the outside world. Encourage them to join professional bodies, write blogs, speak at conferences and network online. Somewhere out there is a creative spark waiting to happen.

Lightning conclusion

All businesses need to grow up. But you need to be careful what barriers are being built as it happens. Be aware of which boundaries are useful, and which are getting in the way. Don't be afraid to take a hammer to the walls that stifle electric conversations.

To dismantle your walls, and break down silos, design your environment to make people mingle, increase talent density faster than business complexity and collaborate freely with customers, competitors and partners. If you manage for a non-hierarchical, open, idea focus, you can become more – not less – creative as you grow.

Sparks to remember

Organisational walls kill electric conversations, block communication and slow decision-making.

Focus on ideas, not the pecking order: make sparks the dominant force in your business.

Encourage your people to develop and network with weak ties – people they don't know so well – the ideas are out there.

Develop an outward-looking culture – look for ways to collaborate with freelancers and organisations.

Dynamite walls to preserve and nurture the rampant creativity of your company's earlier, wilder days.

CLEAR steps to change

Communicate

Send a signal about your thoughts on supreme leadership: gather a group of your most junior people and ask: 'What do you think we could do better around here?'

Learn

Look at your rules, policies, processes and business structure and ask yourself: 'Which of our walls are blocking the development of new ideas?'

Energise

Make a list of the top three walls that are definitely just 'cobwebs' from a previous growth crisis.

Act

Dismantle one of these walls; check to see this worked and improved creativity before moving to the next. Remember: this is not just about efficiency and productivity – it's about increasing electric conversations.

Also:

- Is there a way you could create an 'ideas space' – an opportunity to 'bump into each other'? It doesn't need to be expensive. At Major Players, an innovative London-based recruitment business I worked with, one of the teams organised British high tea one afternoon per week on a revolving basis. Tea, cake and a chance to chat without an agenda. The main thing is to use your imagination to make these opportunities feel creative, informal and fun.

- We all know about the power of networking in business. But when was the last time you organised a networking event for your own people involving key clients, suppliers and people outside your current network? I'm not talking about the run of the mill bonding and booze exercises, which generally produce more hangovers than new ideas, but something that genuinely will challenge and create sparks.

Respond

After you have taken the actions above are there other routes to circulate knowledge and ideas in your team? If so, look to dismantle even more barriers.

10

Encourage collisions
How to spark electric conversations to power collaboration

You'll learn:

■ How the complex, modern world demands collaboration

■ What collaboration is and isn't

■ How to power up collaboration on in your business and team through shared knowledge, diversity of talent and a cooperative mindset

"In the long history of humankind (and animal kind, too) those who learned to collaborate and improvise most effectively have prevailed."
Charles Darwin, English naturalist

The Big Bang

Imagine this email arrived from your boss late on Friday evening:

Re: Next Week's Big Challenge!

Hi,

From Monday I would like you to work collaboratively with 7,000 colleagues from 85 countries. Sadly, you'll have limited powers to influence these people (sorry!). You can't manage them directly;

they actually work for 600 different organisations. For the same reason, you don't have the power to offer them a bonus, recognition outside the office, or more money. But, of course, it's really important all the things they're doing are aligned to a clear plan! You'll be attempting to achieve something that, until recently, most people thought impossible: to smash atoms together at the speed of light to transform our understanding of the universe. As a result, I'm afraid the world's media will be watching! Good luck!

Best wishes

The Boss

This is the managerial challenge facing the men and women who run the Large Hadron Collider (LHC) at the European Organisation for Nuclear Research (CERN) every day. They are attempting to recreate the conditions one-thousandth of a billionth of a second after the beginning of the Universe: the Big Bang. Semi-autonomous teams use the 27-km-long circular tunnel and 4 enormous detectors to inspect particles that emerge from the collisions. The equipment for one of the main experiments, ATLAS, weighs as much as the Eiffel Tower, has about 20 million functional components, uses 3000 kilometres of cables and requires 5 million lines of computing code to run. The majority of CERN is buried up to 100 metres underneath the border between France and Switzerland. Billions of Euros have been invested. This is the biggest science experiment in history.

There's so much at stake, you might expect CERN to be run like a Swiss watch tick-tick-ticking to the iron-rule of directive authority. Actually, the opposite is true. The giant facility is overseen by a director general, but amongst the experimental teams there's no all-powerful authority figure and little hierarchy. There aren't even the usual 'corner office' trappings of individual power. The main physics building is cylindrical; the offices exactly the same size. The leader of each experiment is democratically dubbed the 'spokesperson', and a 'resources coordinator' tracks the allocation of money and people.

Collaboration is imperative. There is a huge amount of information spewing forth from CERN's experiments. To encourage people to work together, CERN offers space and opportunities for everyone to share their ideas. Different perspectives are actively encouraged, not just tolerated. Eight times a year CERN stages a week-long collaboration summit to discuss progress. But electric conversations happen more informally, every day. Markus Nordberg, former resource coordinator for the ATLAS Experiment, told me in his clipped Finnish accent that the big summits are actually rather formal and boring. Teams are most creative in smaller groups: 'The real work happens in the informal collaborative meetings. The probability of you not finding a parking space is very high because we have some sort of meeting going on every day. There is something like 10,000 of them a year. Our cafeteria is the biggest in Geneva, but, if we'd been having lunch today, I'd have had to take you out in the cold. There's so much buzz here it just can't cope.'[1]

With all this freedom it could be chaotic. Nordberg, who's now heading up a special educational programme to bring students, businesses and scientists together to work on and learn about experimental innovation, added: 'We are a bit like blind men in a dark room. We feel our way through. It's a room no one else has ever been in before. We keep our options open. We are absorbing uncertainty, not reducing it. Compared to a normal business this looks like it's on the brink of chaos. Not necessarily chaotic, but almost. But we know how to manage divergence; that's our business.'

Chaos is averted because CERN's scientists are aligned by an enormous sense of purpose. They are inspired by what they are doing. There's also a profound sense of trust generated from a mutual code of ethics: a clear expectation each scientist will work hard and share their knowledge. The community is close-knit with individual success predicated on building a good reputation amongst peers. Anyone who attempts to build a fiefdom, or hoard information, is ostracised. Considering the sums of money invested there is also a remarkable lack of secrecy. CERN publishes all of its findings: you can access the results of each experiment through a public website.[2]

CERN's managerial ethos rejects the idea of the lone genius in favour of a creative system in which talented people are encouraged to rely on each other for inspiration, breakthroughs and ideas. CERN is a potent metaphor for how creative collaboration works. The Large Hadron Collider smashes atoms together in order to sift through the debris for clues to the secrets of the Universe. Creative businesses encourage the collision of knowledge through electric conversations. Within the resulting sparks they search for a profitable new idea.

☀ Throw out any old-fashioned views of creativity being about a lone genius. Build your own Large Hadron Collider: a creative 'system' in which people want to collaborate for a common purpose.

More creative together

Collaboration is more important than ever because of the complexity of modern business problems. Long gone are the days when the CEO had all the good ideas and everyone else put them into practice. A complex, interdependent world requires levels of collaboration never seen before. Just look in your pocket. There is no man or woman on Earth that could recreate all the different technologies in the ubiquitous smart phone.

We work on business systems that are the fruits of collaborative endeavour between thousands of people. Apache, the free open source web server that's won over half the corporate market, is developed and managed by a far flung army of volunteers, most of whom have never met each other.[3] Albert Einstein's famous remark, 'We cannot solve our problems with the same thinking we used when we created them,' now has gone a step further. We can no longer improve on existing technologies with the same thinking – or, without the help of each other.

Collaboration is as old as business itself. After all, people working together is what distinguishes an organisation from the lone inventor working out of his or her back bedroom. The legendary Henry Ford said: 'If everyone is moving forward together, then success takes care of itself.' But creative collaboration is very different from his philosophy for car manufacturing. 'Fordism' was about thousands of people working together under tightly prescribed conditions of scientific management to produce uniform products. Creative collaboration is how people can work together to produce the opposite: new ideas.

Collaboration isn't ...

It's good to know what collaboration **isn't**.

It's not about competition

Competition between people and teams sounds like a good idea. Statements like: 'We encourage people to compete with each other to drive ingenuity' feel good. Competition is what makes business tick, right? Wrong. Competition works brilliantly to winnow out the best products for consumers and it motivates employees in individualistic sales roles: bond traders, car salesmen, telesales operators and the like.

It even works for creativity – but only if it is limited in time and scope. For example, Paul Kitcatt, co-founder and creative director of the digital agency Kitcatt Nohr Digitas, pitched seven creative teams against each other to develop ideas in the run up to a major client pitch for the supermarket Waitrose. But the competition was contained. Before the pitch, Kitcatt managed a group creative review, where all the teams were encouraged to step away from their own work and critique the different ideas brought into the room. He avoids dictating what's 'good' or 'bad', but instead encourages those around him to put the quality of ideas above hierarchy and their own ego. To such an extent, a horrified freelance account handler, who observed the creative review, told Kitcatt's business partner: 'It looks like Communism!' Reflecting on the session, Kitcatt commented: 'I thought there were two or three things that we could develop and the rest we could get rid of. But they had already agreed that amongst themselves. So, I really didn't need to say anything; they know what's good. I genuinely believe people know quality if you let them think about it.' Kitcatt's agency won the account. The account handler later texted: 'Communism works!'

Research shows that too much competition amongst people **on the same team** leads to a sterile transactional mindset: 'I will give you A, only if you offer B in return'. This might work for estate agents, but it's poisonous when people need to think together, share knowledge and build on each other's ideas. Interestingly, London Business School's Lynda Gratton found companies with a cooperative attitude also often had an active corporate social responsibility programme. It seems the concept of giving with no thought for reciprocal gain is infectious.[4]

☀ Use limited and contained competition to add spice to electric conversations between teams. But don't forget: adding competition to creative projects is like seasoning soup. Too much salt, the dish is ruined.

It's not about consensus building

Encouraging collaboration requires a different mindset to political consensus building. The following table shows how collaboration impacts on organisational structure, information sharing and performance measurement. It is the opposite of a command-and-control style of leadership; but equally it's not politicking either.

	Command and control	Consensus	Collaborative
Business structure	A hierarchy	A matrix or small group	A network across the business
Who has information?	Senior management	Chosen people	Employees at all levels
Who makes decisions?	People at the top	All parties	People leading projects
How do you measure performance?	Financial results against plan	Lots of different performance indicators	Shared goals
Where does it work best?	When a business has clear and simple goals	Small teams, but it is slow	Collaborative businesses when creativity is key

Adapted from Ibarra, H. and Hansen, M.T., 'Are you a collaborative leader?', *Harvard Business Review*, July 2011

Switching on collaboration

There are four powerful approaches to collaboration in your business or team:

1 Electric conversations.

2 Shared knowledge.

3 Talent cocktails.

4 A collaborative attitude.

1 Electric conversations

"Everyone has an idea. But it's really about executing the idea and attracting other people to help you work on the idea."
Jack Welch, former chairman and CEO of General Electric[5]

Electric conversations power collaboration. David Sproxton CBE is a quiet, cerebral man who also happens to be the chairman of a world-famous animation studio: Aardman. Based in Bristol, Aardman Animations is the birthplace of a peculiarly British duo of animated movie characters, Wallace & Gromit. Sproxton allows his intuition and awareness of electric conversations to act as a guide to his leadership. He said: 'A creative atmosphere is about conversations. What are people talking about? What's the buzz? In a way, general chit chat. Are they excited when you mention certain subjects, certain topics, certain projects? It's a bit like playground chatter, isn't it? What's the buzz, what's trending?, as they say these days. What's turning people on; what are they anxious about?'[6] Electric conversations are different from a lot of 'normal' business talk, which can feel like an energy-free dialogue between an overbearing boss and a nervous employee. Much business communication can be overshadowed by hierarchy, rather than the quality of the ideas in question.

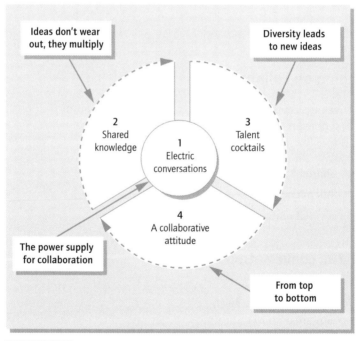

figure 10.1   Four powerful approaches to increasing collaboration

☀ Build a strong – but not necessarily always 'comfortable' – relationship with your team members.

Cut the crap

"Only dead fish go with the flow."
Malcolm Muggeridge, English journalist

Electric conversations involve genuinely listening to – and building upon – other people's ideas. But they aren't about being polite. Co-founder of Polaroid Edwin Land stated it plainly: 'Politeness is the poison of collaboration.' The global advertising agency Ogilvy & Mather exhort staff to avoid the 'tyranny of politeness': 'We are a company of problem solvers. Our job requires us to be brutally honest and dedicated to the truth. For, unless we know the truth, in all its unlovely details, how are we to go about the business of problem solving? If we avoid candour in order to curry favour with other people, we actually destroy trust. If someone asks us for our opinion and we don't offer it, our answer is not only dishonest, it's worthless. We only get a spark when the stone and the flint are moving in opposite directions.'[7]

☀ Build your own Large Hadron Collider: a creative 'system' in which people want to collaborate for a common purpose.

In February 2002, Greg Dyke had been director general of the British public broadcaster BBC for two years. He knew the licence-fee-funded 'Auntie Beeb' was underperforming.[8] Dyke was determined to shake things up a little. He knew that, to improve, the BBC needed to be braver, more creative and less bureaucratic. In a speech to BBC employees to mark his second anniversary at the head of the corporation, he said his mission was to turn the broadcaster into a 'can-do' organisation: 'the most innovative and risk-taking place there is'.

To send a clear message about the value of electric conversations, he launched an extraordinary initiative. Yellow cards appeared in meeting rooms across the business. Yellow cards come from English football. The referee brandishes one to warn a player for breaking the rules. If you get two yellow cards, you're off the pitch. In BBC meetings, if a great idea was being stifled, staffers were encouraged to grab one of the cards and show it to the person getting in the way. On the card was a simple message: 'Cut the crap and make it happen'.

Electric conversations value relationships, but not at the expense of ideas. The intention is to work together for the best outcome, not a warm, comfortable compromise. They are founded on strong relationships. Confident people create trust and a feeling of safety to try new things. They feel secure enough to disagree, because they know the relationship can withstand the creative friction. Trust and familiarity are key characteristics of a creative team, but so is candour and honesty.

☀ Show people respect, but avoid the tyranny of politeness.

2 Shared knowledge

Ideas are inexhaustible. In 1813, American Founding Father and the third President of the USA, Thomas Jefferson, wrote: 'He who receives an idea from me, receives instruction himself without lessening mine; as he who lights his taper at mine, receives light without darkening me.'[9]

In 1990, the economist Paul Romer added scientific rigour to Jefferson's inspiring wisdom. Romer argues that, while economics is based on the concept of scarce resources, ideas are 'non-rival good'. In other words, as Jefferson spotted, when ideas are used, they don't wear out – they create lots of little new ideas. Romer added: 'The thing about ideas is that they naturally inspire new ones. This is why places that facilitate idea sharing tend to become more productive and innovative than those that don't. Because when ideas are shared, the possibilities do not add up. They multiply.'[10] This is why creative businesses share knowledge like it's a hot potato: moving ideas around increases the chance of an inspiring collision.

Creative businesses are also fast learners. Peter Senge in his seminal business book *The Fifth Discipline, The Art and Practice of The Learning Organisation*, argues: 'The only sustainable competitive advantage is an organisation's ability to learn faster than the competition.'[11] Creative businesses need to learn fast and collaborate to succeed. There are two different types of knowledge to share. Understanding them both helps you to work out the best plan to disseminate knowledge across your business or team:

■ **Explicit knowledge**: This is knowledge that can be written down, stored and distributed: client information, new briefs, interesting trends and competitor information. Wikipedia is a good example of how explicit knowledge has been shared to the benefit of millions.

■ **Tacit knowledge**: This is knowledge that is in people's heads, the stuff they can't clearly codify. It is more difficult to share because you can't write it down. Sometimes people aren't even aware of the knowledge they have – or how valuable it might be to others. Tacit knowledge often emerges only in face-to-face conversations.

※ Choose the right mixture of communication, technology and management policies to share the maximum amount of explicit **and** tacit knowledge.

Knowledge sharing

Some knowledge-sharing policies distribute both tacit and explicit knowledge. But not all, as Figure 10.2 explains. All of the

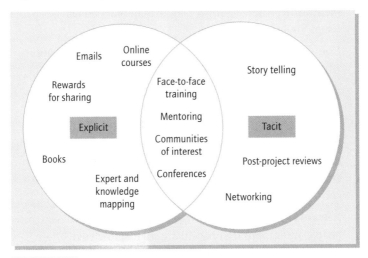

figure 10.2 **Some knowledge-sharing ideas**

explicit knowledge-sharing ideas can be made to work harder and smarter using the explosion of online technologies now available – file sharing, collaborative working tools, intranets, databases and social networking.

☀ **Share tacit knowledge by encouraging 'random', water-cooler moments. Share explicit knowledge through formal policies, media and online networking.**

Tacit knowledge crops up in electric conversations. When two people share their experience, stories and insights – the stuff they often didn't even realise was that important. Ping! new ideas multiply. Here are a few of the many ways to share knowledge in your business:

- **Face-to-face training**: Formal training from outside experts – as well as internal learning seminars bring together different teams to transfer best practice.

- **Mentoring**: Pairing two people based on one person's knowledge and experience in a specific area and the other person's appetite and need to learn. It can be as formal as an apprenticeship. Traditional mentoring has a senior/junior dynamic to it. But many businesses now organise 'reverse mentoring', where younger people help older colleagues with issues, such as social media.

- **Communities of interest**: On- and offline groups of people who share a craft or a profession inside and outside the business. The group can evolve naturally, or can be created with a specific goal.

- **Conferences**: This route includes away days and knowledge fairs to help people and ideas to come together. Don't forget to think about inviting customers and suppliers. Encourage employees to get out of the business to learn from external conferences and exhibitions.

- **Rewards for sharing**: Review your reward system to recognise people and groups that habitually share knowledge.

■ **Expert and knowledge mapping**: Use online tools and databases to connect those who know with those who don't know.

■ **After-action reviews**: Analyse what happened, why it happened, and how it can be done better.

■ **Knowledge brokers**: Guaranteed to speed up the movement of ideas around the business. Saatchi & Saatchi took this role seriously. Worldwide deputy chairman Richard Hytner's job is to help all other employees in the 5,000-person business to understand Saatchi & Saatchi's dream, beliefs, spirit and creative focus.

■ **A department of surprises**: That's what The Body Shop founder Anita Roddick once said she'd like to create. The giant oil company Royal Dutch/Shell created its own: autonomous teams of six people – called GameChangers – based across the world hunting for new ideas. The teams have the power to allocate up to $20 million to trial good ideas when they find them. It works. These groups have created more than half of Shell's innovations.[12]

☀ Tell war stories: as a way to share explicit knowledge, build a collaborative culture and develop a shared understanding of the risks and rewards of the creative process, storytelling is difficult to beat.

3 Mix talent cocktails

Collaboration is improved by the diversity of the people around the table. In September 2013, the mobile phone business of Nokia was sold to Microsoft. In Finland, Nokia's homeland, this was seen as a national disaster. For decades Nokia had pioneered the mobile phone boom. Its fortunes began to fall soon after Apple introduced the iPhone in 2007. But many people still believed it would make a comeback. They were wrong. Nokia's shares slumped by more than 80 per cent in the following years.[13] Ironic, as Nokia was way ahead of the innovation game in the early

2000s, but its best ideas were stifled for years within a bureaucratic and insular culture. The company was based in Helsinki, a world away from the technology Mecca of Silicon Valley. In mid-2011 management realised its mistake and moved the HQ to Palo Alto, in California.[14] But perhaps location was not the biggest factor. The root of Nokia's inability to innovate can be traced right back to the boardroom. The executive team had worked together for over a decade, and they had one thing in common: they were all Finnish. Many people believe it was this bland cultural uniformity – and the resulting cosiness of their team – that lead to them to wilfully ignore the competitive threat. They had fallen victim to group think.

Group think is when teams make worse decisions together than they would as individuals. They isolate themselves from outside influences. The attitude becomes: 'If we don't know it already, it's not worth knowing'. The more cohesive the group, the more likely it is that they will fall into the trap. The team self-censors ideas that deviate from group consensus and offer the illusion of unanimity, even to themselves (a person's silence is viewed as agreement). Those who oppose the group are seen as biased, weak or even spiteful. Pressure to conform will be placed on members who question the group, often accompanied by accusations of 'disloyalty'.

☀ Mix talent cocktails to keep collaborations fresh. Bland teams with the same experience, skills and background exert a pressure towards uniformity which stifles original thought.

The Q factor: diversity rules

Clues to avoiding group think can be found in the Q factor of your business. Brian Uzzi, a sociologist at Northwestern University in Illinois, has spent a career analysing the ideal relationships required to produce effective collaborations. He stumbled upon Broadway musicals as a proxy for creative business projects. Like any new product, musicals need to be original, popular and commercially successful. Like a business, musicals also have to bring together different disciplines. Instead of accountants, website engineers and project managers, think lyricists, choreographers, actors, directors and producers.

Uzzi set out to investigate the ideal relationship between people trying to work together creatively. It was a mammoth task. He spent five years analysing all the Broadway musicals between 1877 and 1990 – a total of 2,258 shows. His discovered that theatre land in New York is an extremely interconnected world. Everybody knows everybody. His second insight was the social intimacy between people – how **well** they know each other – plays a major part in how successful the show will be. He called it the Q Factor: a measure of how densely connected the whole Broadway musical community was at any one time. He then correlated the Q factor across all the musicals he analysed. The results are fascinating for anyone managing a team for creative results:

- When the Q score is **low** – people don't know each other well – the musicals are far more likely to fail. People in the system haven't built up sufficient trust to collaborate successfully with each other.

- When the Q score is **high** – people know each other very well – the musicals are also likely to bomb. Teams are so comfortable with each other, they all think alike.

- The best musicals by far were produced by teams in years when the Q scores were in the **middle** – when people knew each other well enough to have formed a common language, but have not become so close to have lost their edge. These teams were 2.5 times more likely to hit the commercial jackpot with their shows – 3 times more likely to be loved by the critics.

Uzzi said: 'The best Broadway teams, by far, were those with a mix of relationships. These teams had some old friends, but they also had newbies. This mixture means the artists could interact efficiently – they had a familiar structure to fall back on – but they also managed to incorporate some new ideas. They were comfortable with each other, but they weren't too comfortable.'[15] Uzzi's work is supported by a battery of research, which shows teams with a diverse range of ages, ethnic backgrounds, skill sets and attitudes perform better than teams that all look, sound and think the same.

※ Manage your team to be like Goldilocks' porridge
– not too familiar with each other, not too unfamiliar –
right on the edge between the two. It's proven this l
eads to more creative **and** profitable outcomes.

Start by looking at your own management team – this needs to
lead by example. Reckitt Benckiser is a UK-based producer of
home and health products: making everything from Airwick
to Cillit Bang. In 1999, Reckitt Benckiser had around 20,000
employees, produced net revenues of just over £3 billion with an
operating profit of £357 million. Fourteen years later, the company has more than tripled its revenues to £9.5 billion. Profits
went up 200 per cent, while headcount rose by just 75 per cent.
One factor in this success story is the diversity of the leadership
team. Retired Dutch CEO Bart Brecht said: 'It doesn't matter
whether I have a Pakistani, a Chinese person, a Brit, or a Turk,
a man or a woman, sitting in the same room, or whether I have
people from sales or something else, so long as I have people with
different experiences – because the chance for new ideas is much
greater when you have people with different backgrounds. The
chance for conflict is also higher – and conflict is good per se, as
long as it's constructive and gets us to the best idea.'[16] The diversity policy has been continued under new Indian CEO, Rakesh
Kapoor. Kapoor's executive committee of nine contains eight
different nationalities: British, Indian, South African, Belgian,
Canadian, Italian, Brazilian and Dutch. This isn't about political
correctness: nationalities represent different points of view.

Ensure your team is a talent cocktail: people from different professional and ethnic backgrounds – and 'outsiders' from different
parts of your business. Younger people are natural outsiders; in
business older people are too these days. Sometimes, even inviting people with no experience in the area being discussed can
help. For example, a digital agency I worked with routinely ran
creative ideas past the finance team.

Electric labs

A fast way to experiment with diversity is by setting up your own
electric laboratory. These are not traditional R&D departments

because they are not permanent. They're set up for a limited amount of time. A company can create an electric lab simply by putting some time and space aside for a group of people from different disciplines to work together on a particular project that requires some creative thought. You won't be alone:

■ Procter & Gamble is one of many enlightened business that realises this is worth the investment of time. It created its Clay Street Project, which is a refurbished five-storey town house in Cincinnati in which cross-functional teams spend 10 weeks together working on new brands.

■ Toy manufacturer Mattel runs Project Platypus, which throws together a group of around 12 to 20 employees from different corners of the business for three months. They are put in a temporary office, which they can set up with movable furniture. They have access to resources, materials and toys. The challenge is for the team to develop new products. Rival Fisher-Price has a similar approach – it calls its innovation lab The Cave.

■ Motorola also developed the ultra-thin Razr mobile phone range this way.

■ Sony turned to a lab technique when it realised its organisational silos were blocking electric conversations between engineers and designers.

☀ Found your own electric lab. They work in companies large or small. You don't need a purpose-built facility. Just a room, some design materials and people who are from different areas of your business.

4 A collaborative attitude

IDEO (pronounced 'eye-dee-oh') is an award-winning global design firm that helps organisations to innovate and grow. To unleash the extraordinarily high levels of creativity they need, they've made collaborative generosity the norm: they call it a 'culture of helping'. CEO Tim Brown said: 'The more complex the problem, the more help you need. And that's the stuff we're being asked to tackle.' A team of Harvard professors mapped the social networks at IDEO and came up with some crucial insights:

- **Leader conviction**: Leaders and managers need to lose their ego and ask for help themselves – this makes it the norm to get help from other people without feeling like you're 'in debt'. Management must also reinforce the idea of helping through formal processes and job descriptions.

- **A dense network**: To encourage collaboration you need to develop a dense network of mutual assistance across the business – it can't just be the same people helping out every time.

- **Slack in schedules**: You are more likely to help someone else if you aren't permanently up to your eyeballs in work. Management needs to build in downtime for people to help others.

Interestingly, the analysis also revealed those rated most helpful are not necessarily the most technically competent – but they are seen as the most trustworthy and accessible. The good Samaritan doesn't just need to be knowledgeable; he or she needs to be good at the art of helping. At AT&T Labs, the famously inventive research and development division of the US telecoms business, management wanted to find out why some individuals were more creative than others. They found one astounding common thread. Workers with the most patents to their name often shared breakfast or lunch with a certain electrical engineer called Harry Nyquist. As it turned out, Harry was particularly skilled at asking good questions.[17]

The 'unwritten rules'

A collaborative attitude needs to be amplified through your unwritten rules. This is behaviour that's not codified, but comes through loud and clear for any new employee on their first day in the job. Does the person find there's a prevailing attitude success comes from collaboration? Or, do people whisper about being 'at war' with other departments? In her study of innovative commercial 'hotspots' London Business School's Lynda Gratton concluded that a foundation stone for increased creativity was the existence of 'a cooperative mindset'.[18]

To be successful, collaboration needs to start at the top. Leaders need to 'walk the talk'. They need to make it clear through words and deeds that the company expects employees to help each other. This was confirmed by a *Harvard Business Review* study of over 2,000 CEOs: leaders reported that they knew they needed to offer a positive example to staff by demonstrating collaboration amongst the management team first.[19]

☀ Lead by example – collaboration spreads when people at the top go first.

Participation in big decisions

People work together better when they know what mountain they are trying to climb. You can send a persuasive sign that you are serious about collaboration if you invite people to help choose the mountain in the first place. I work with leaders to make strategy development as inclusive as it can be. Handled well, inviting employees to contribute to debates around shared goals, organisational purpose and values leads to better decisions and vastly increased buy-in.

Some companies take the idea of employee power even further. Ricardo Semler often clashed with his father, Antonio, about the management style of Semco, their family-owned Brazilian manufacturing business. The father and son's philosophy could not have been more different. Ricardo favoured a decentralised approach in which workers were empowered to take decisions; Antonio believed in a traditional autocratic style of management. After countless arguments, in 1980, aged just 21, Ricardo took over from his father to become CEO.

At the time, Semco had a hundred employees and $4 million in revenues – as well as being on the verge of bankruptcy. To save the business, Ricardo knew he needed to do something radical. He certainly had a first day to remember: he fired 60 per cent of the company's managers. He then slashed bureaucracy to create a truly collaborative company in which knowledge was shared with all employees. Most radically of all, Ricardo handed workers the keys to the boardroom. From day one they had a big say in key decisions. To make this work, the business avoided long-term planning, preferring to look only six months ahead. It worked. In the next 20 years, Semco grew faster than almost every other company in Brazil. By 2003, revenues had grown from $4 million to $212 million. In the same year, the business threw a big party to celebrate the tenth anniversary of the last time Ricardo made a decision on his own.[20]

Most leaders are wary of going this far down the road in giving employees a voice. My advice is, be brave, at least take a few steps. Occasionally, when I've encouraged business leaders to talk to their staff about the big picture, the executive response has been: 'Why ask where we should be going? That's what I'm paid for!' This shows a lack of confidence. Leaders who are comfortable with their authority are happy to listen as they know they have nothing to lose. A more engaging, transparent strategy development process does not abdicate responsibility. Employees don't join a business expecting one person – one vote. But they do appreciate being consulted. If this is done with skill – enlisting an experienced external facilitator is a good idea – the result is vastly more buy-in when the plans are implemented. I've been involved in many strategy review processes. The discussions are inspiring and of a high quality: true electric conversations about the future.

※ Make clear how much influence your employees actually have. When 'empowerment' is just a smokescreen – with no intention to listen – it causes legitimate resentment.

A strong hand

The downside of collaboration is that sometimes people get the idea it's more important than results or good ideas. This creates 'talking shop' meetings, endlessly debating ideas and struggling to find consensus. The counterintuitive aspect of collaborative leadership is it involves being decisive when required. After there has been a debate, a manager should help move people from talk to action. It's great to challenge, it's brilliant to debate, but at a certain point something needs to get done. As the Persian leader Cyrus the Great wrote in 530 BC: 'Diversity in counsel, unity in command.'

Electric conclusion

Without collaborations powered by electric conversations, a creative business is just lots of people working inside the same building. Successful creative collaboration of diverse, cross-functional teams, using the unique knowledge within your business is the crowning step of our journey. But, as with all of the 10 habits of business creativity: it has to start with you.

Sparks to remember

➤ Collaboration is more important than ever because of the complexity of modern-day business problems.

➤ Collaboration will be encouraged or killed, dependent on the attitude and actions of leaders – this feeds into the unwritten rules of the business.

➤ Collaboration is not about consensus building – and will be discouraged by too much competition inside teams.

➤ Collaboration should be reflected in everything from organisational structure to how decisions get made.

➤ Creative businesses are transparent about information – they ensure explicit and tacit knowledge is shared as widely as possible.

CLEAR steps to change

Communicate

Arrange a coffee with a member of your team that represents a different 'tribe' in your business. Discuss all the different ways you could share explicit and tacit knowledge.

Learn

Ask yourself: how collaborative is my leadership style? Then ask the same question to the people who report into you. Compare the answers.

Energise

Think about the most important team in your business. It might be the management team, the business development team or the production department. How diverse are they as a group of people in terms of their personal styles, backgrounds and experience? How could you refresh the team to keep them at their most creative?

Think how you might improve the flow of knowledge in your business or team. Use the list in the chapter above, but don't confine yourself to that – there's plenty more.

Act

Experiment with team collaboration in implementing the themes in this book. Pick the habit you think is most crucial to your business and put together a diverse A-Team to discuss the approaches in the habit and what might work for your business.

Respond

Take this as a useful moment at the end of the 10 habits to review all the **CLEAR** exercises and work out which ones you need to return to.

Ten creative business myths debunked

"If you never change your mind, why have one?"
Edward de Bono

I wrote this book to help people who want to boost innovation in their business. One obstacle is that business creativity is shrouded in unhelpful myths. The folklore gets in the way of leaders thinking clearly about how their teams and people can be more creative. Managing for ideas is full of intriguing tensions; but there's no reason to add more complexity. My mission is to simplify. So, here's some clarity on some popular untruths about commercial creativity.[1]

Myth 1 Brainstorming works best

Advertising legend Alex Osborn (one of the Bs in the global agency BBDO) invented brainstorming in the 1940s. Osborn boasted that brainstorming doubles the quantity of ideas from any group. He stipulated two rules:

1   **Everyone in the group should get involved**: Throwing in ideas in an explosion of almost random thoughts. The thinking is, if you sift through sufficient quantities of grit, mud and dirt, eventually you will find glistening nuggets of gold. He advised groups to: '...focus on quantity. Quality will come later.'

2   **Participants must avoid negative feedback on what they
    hear**: The assumption is that people will not risk embarrassing
    themselves if they are likely to hear their idea being trashed by
    others. Osborn called creativity a 'delicate flower'.

Brainstorming is now the most popular creative technique of all
time. It is used in advertising offices and design firms, the class-
room and the boardroom. But there's a small problem. It doesn't
work. A famous test in 1958 found people working alone came
up with a far greater **quantity** of ideas (twice as many); their
solutions were also of a higher **quality**. It turns out that brainstorming has the opposite effect on people panhandling for
ideas: they find less gold, and the gold they do find is of an infe-
rior quality. It speaks volumes about the state of creativity in
modern business that brainstorming is a dud. It means the limited amount of time companies devote to being creative is not
being managed effectively. It's worth saying this again; it is, after
all, quite startling:

- Creativity is the root of all new ideas and profits.
- Most businesses don't spend enough time and energy on
  being creative.
- When they do, they use a technique that doesn't work as well
  as the most obvious alternative.

It's as if we were running modern businesses on a 1940s size-
of-a-room Bakelite computer with less processing power than
a modern wristwatch. Worldwide deputy chairman of Saatchi
& Saatchi Richard Hytner acknowledges the reservations about
brainstorming but still uses it with his teams and with clients: 'I'm a fan of brainstorming. I think the reason it's become
debased is because the people running the brainstorms have run
out of ideas, run out of juice. Brainstorming at its best is where
people are really skilfully facilitated.'[2]

I would still advise you to use brainstorming with teams. Not
because it is the most efficient way to come up with ideas;
but because it encourages people to collaborate and engage in
non-judgemental electric conversations. One warning: make sure

to practise your facilitation skills first – brainstorming needs a listening and skilled group leader who understands the divergent-convergent nature of the creative process (see Habit 2 Break the management rules).

☀ Forget the myth, but embrace the positives of brainstorming.

Myth 2 You need to be a genius

People touched by genius dominate our perception of creativity: Albert Einstein, Charles Dickens, Charlotte Brontë, Ernest Hemingway, William Shakespeare, Michelangelo, da Vinci and Picasso. The way their life stories get told often perpetuate the idea that creativity is the preserve of a handful of slightly unhinged titans. The mythology of creativity being the sole preserve of the lone genius goes back a long way in Western thought – from Plato's 'divine madness' through Romanticism and Freudian psychoanalysis. Clearly, some people are very gifted. But that should not act as a stop sign for others. Academic Robert Weisberg analysed the genius myth of Mozart, Picasso and Coleridge and argues that their stunning achievements can be explained through logical progressions, memory, training, opportunity and hard work.[3] Malcolm Gladwell provides even more context with 'Outliers', his study of the factors that contribute to success. Taking Bill Gates and The Beatles as examples, he argues success in any field is often a matter of practising a specific task for a long time. The magic number, according to Gladwell's research, is 10,000 hours. That's eight hours a day for about five years.[4]

☀ To become innovative in a particular business sphere, first work hard to master your craft.

Myth 3 You need to be very clever

Intelligence correlates with creativity only to a point. And, it's a fairly modest point at that. To put this into context, two-thirds of us have an IQ between 85 to 115, and the average IQ in an

industrialised country is 100.[5] The ability to be creative is positively correlated with IQ only up to an IQ of 120. Above that the
link evaporates.

☀ If you're intelligent enough to read this book,
you can be very creative indeed.

Myth 4 You're either creative, or you're not

The 'myth of the genius' also leads to a general condemnation by
some of any techniques or approaches to help 'normal' people
to develop a more creative attitude. This isn't useful, as far as I'm
concerned. Clearly, some people are brighter than others. Some
people will run the 100 metres faster than 99.9 per cent of the
population, however hard the rest of us train. That's life. And,
some people are more creative than others. Business should
try to hire as many of these creative powerhouses as they can.
Meanwhile, we should all try to develop a more creative outlook
on life – and develop what gifts we have.

☀ Think about your career and work out when
you were creative – and what opportunities you
might have missed. How can you be more creative
inside and outside work – as well as encouraging
creativity in those around you?

Myth 5 All businesses must be creative all of the time

All businesses can benefit from being able to encourage more
creative ideas from their people. But no business can be creative
100 per cent of the time. That would be ridiculous. It will always
be a balance between exploiting well-trodden processes and
proven products and investing time and resources in developing
new ideas.

☀ Work out when and where you would like the creative sparks to fly:

1 agree the time in the business cycle your people need to be at their most creative – and when it's 'all about delivery';

2 identify the teams that need to have a more creative attitude than the rest of your business.

Myth 6 Creativity belongs to the young

Creativity often comes from outsiders, people who don't know how things 'should be done'. The young are naturally sceptical of the status quo. But age is not a predictor for creativity. Counter-intuitively, it is expertise that inhibits it. Experts find it difficult to see or think outside the patterns they have learned. The tragedy is that our school system seems to want to produce expert minds, rather than creative ones. Creativity and education expert Sir Ken Robinson tells the story of a little girl busily sketching in class when her teacher stops next to her desk to ask what she's drawing. 'It's a picture of God,' the girl says. The teacher patiently explains that nobody knows what God looks like. 'They will in a minute,' the girl replies. It's a shame most of us have that kind of creative confidence knocked out of us.

☀ Shake things up by inviting people into projects who have no experience in the area being discussed – they won't be constrained by how things normally get done.

Myth 7 Creativity is a solitary act

When we think of creativity we see Van Gogh in his Parisian garret, Archimedes in his bath and William Wordsworth wandering lonely as a cloud sniffing the odd daffodil. But, as I've argued in this book business creativity is by definition a team sport. And the increasing complexity of the modern world means creative collaboration is required more than ever before. The myth states that creativity is for individuals, not a team.

☀ Embrace the fact more and more of the world's new products come from creative collaborations. This is only likely to increase.

Myth 8 You can't manage creativity

Creativity doesn't respond to many people's perceptions of traditional hierarchical management. True. Organisational culture plays a big part in encouraging creativity. But there are managerial interventions to lead the culture in the right way – see Habit 7 Build a business playground. Also, management skills make it easier for ideas to get a fair hearing and be developed further. Practise the approaches in Habit 2 Break the management rules.

☀ Leadership and management makes a big difference. And it can be positive, or very destructive, to business creativity.

Myth 9 Creativity will happen only in 'creative departments'

This is the idea that creativity can happen only in marketing or R&D teams – or at the offices of your advertising agency. Of course, businesses will always have some teams that are hotspots for creativity. And ideas do need a special climate to grow. But, one of the biggest barriers to break down in any business is the one in peoples' **minds** – the barrier between who is creative and who isn't. It's the same rationale that means everyone should be aware of the bottom line, whether they are an accountant or not. Creativity is too valuable to be left to the experts!

☀ Encourage everyone in all departments to approach their work in a creative way.

Myth 10 It's important to distinguish between 'applied' and 'pure' creativity

There are agonised and divisive debates in the halls of academia about the nature of creativity. The divide is around the difference between problem solving: what often happens in business, connected with intelligence and reasoning – what could be called applied creativity and pure creativity: what artists do, connected with the unconscious aha! moment that creeps up on you and then announces itself. Pure creativity is cartoonist Matt Groening inventing the idea of the Simpsons in 1987.[6] Applied creativity is the writing and animation teams trying to make it funny and relevant 25 years later after 500-plus episodes.

I have not got bogged down in this because it's not a valuable distinction for the real-life leaders of businesses I work with. There are specific problems to be solved: everything from responding to a client brief, to improving how a production line runs, to developing a new product. And there are creative leaps: the so-called aha! moments. Aha! moments produce solutions to problems 'we never knew we had'. In the arts world we have the *Mona Lisa*, *Don Quixote* and *The Great Gatsby*. But, transformative pure-creativity solutions to problems we never knew we had also crop up in business: Pixar's *Toy Story*, Kindle's e-reader, the bar code, self-service supermarkets, Velcro and Google, to name a few. One thing is certain: people tend to make huge profits if they manage to innovate and commercialise good ideas. Human creativity plays its part in both pure and applied creativity. Both are highly valuable and lead to innovation and new revenues.

☀ Practise the organisational and managerial habits in *The Spark*. They will encourage pure and applied creativity.

Notes

Introduction

1   Afshar, V., 2013. 100 Tweetable Business Culture Quotes from Brilliant Executives [online]. Available at: <www.huffingtonpost.com/vala-afshar/100-tweetable-business-cu_b_3575595.html>.

Habit 1 Start an electric conversation

1   Caponigro, J.P., 2013. *25 Quotes on Creativity* [online]. Available at: <www.johnpaulcaponigro.com/blog/11317/25-quotes-on-creativity/#sthash.XGJzLxR0.dpuf>.

2   Thanks to Gordon Torr.

3   Csikszentmihalyi, M., 2002. *Flow*. London: Rider. p.4.

4   Sawyer, K., 2007. *Group genius: The creative power of collaboration*. New York, NY: Basic Books.

Habit 2 Break the management rules

1   *Creative Quotes and Quotations on Managing* [online]. Available at: <http://creatingminds.org/quotes/managing.htm>.

2   Murphy, S., 2013. Interviewed by Greg Orme at Sky Grant Way, Isleworth on 29 August.

3   Kiechel III, W., 2012. The management century. *Harvard Business Review*, November.

4   Taylor, F.W., 1911. *The principles of scientific management*. New York and London: Harper & Brothers.

5   Sutton, R.I., 2001. The weird rules of creativity. *Harvard Business Review*, September, p.96.

6   Long Lingo, E. of Vanderbilt University in Tennessee and O'Mahony, S. of the University of California reported in Amabile, T.M. and Khaire, M., 2008. Creativity and the role of the leader. *Harvard Business Review*, October. Available at: <http://hbr.org/2008/10/creativity-and-the-role-of-the-leader/ar/1>.

7   Amabile, T.M. and Khaire, M., 2008. Creativity and the role of the leader. *Harvard Business Review*, October. Available at: <http://hbr.org/2008/10/creativity-and-the-role-of-the-leader/ar/1>.

8   Hytner, R., 2013. Interviewed by Greg Orme at Saatchi & Saatchi, London, 26 September.

9 Amabile, T.M. and Khaire, M., 2008. Creativity and the role of the leader. *Harvard Business Review*, October. Available at: <http://hbr.org/2008/10/creativity-and-the-role-of-the-leader/ar/1>.

10 The concept of 'The Maze' is featured in Amabile, T.M., 1998. How to kill creativity. *Harvard Business Review*, September.

11 Lehrer, J., 2012. *Imagine: how creativity works*. New York: Houghton Mifflin Harcourt. p. 56.

12 Bilton, C., 2007. *Management and creativity*. Oxford: Blackwell Publishing. p. 9.

Habit 3 Lead with creative choices

1 Hegarty, J., 2013. Interviewed by Greg Orme at BBH London on 24 June.

2 Drucker, P.F., 2008. *The essential Drucker: the best of sixty years of Peter Drucker's essential writings on management*. New York: HarperBusiness.

3 Carr, A., 2010. The most important leadership quality for CEOs? Creativity. *Fast Company* [online]. Available at: <www.fastcompany.com/1648943/most-important-leadership-quality-ceos-creativity>.

4 Robinson, K., 2011. Ken Robinson on the principles of creative leadership. *Fast Company* [online]. Available at: <www.fastcompany.com/1764044/ken-robinson-principles-creative-leadership>.

5 Catliff, N., 2013. Nick Catliff, managing director at Lion TV, interviewed by Greg Orme on 21 May.

6 Goffee, R. and Jones, G., 2006. *Why should anyone be led by you? What it takes to be an authentic leader*. Boston, MA: Harvard Business Press Books.

7 With thanks to Heifetz, R.A. and Linsky, M., 2002. *Leadership on the line: staying alive through the dangers of leading*. Boston, MA: Harvard Business School Press.

8 Goffee, R. and Jones, G., 2006. *Why should anyone be led by you? What it takes to be an authentic leader*. Boston, MA: Harvard Business Press Books. p.29.

9 Ibid.

10 Inspired by Covey, S.R., *The seven habits of highly effective people*, New York, NY: Simon & Schuster, 1989.

11 Judy Rees.

12 Amabile, T.M. and Khaire, M., 2008. Creativity and the role of the leader. *Harvard Business Review*, October. Available at: <http://hbr. org/2008/10/creativity-and-the-role-of-the-leader/ar/1>.

13 Murphy, S., 2013. Interviewed by Greg Orme at Sky Grant Way, Isleworth on 29 August.

14 Capodagli, B. and Jackson, L., 2009. *Innovate the Pixar way: business lessons from the world's most creative corporate playground.* McGraw-Hill Professional.

15 Kitcatt, P., 2013. Interviewed by Greg Orme, 1 October.

16 Ogilvy & Mather, 2009. *The eternal pursuit of unhappiness: being very good is no good, you have to be very, very, very, very, very good.* Ogilvy & Mather Worldwide. p.45.

17 *Business & Finance* [online], quoted in: <http://thelearnersway. net/ideas/2013/3/31/google-reader-skeumorphism-games-apps-and-schools>.

18 Olins, W. 2013. Interviewed by Greg Orme at the Saffron HQ in London, 22 May.

19 Ogilvy & Mather, 2009. *The eternal pursuit of unhappiness: being very good is no good, you have to be very, very, very, very, very good.* Ogilvy & Mather Worldwide. p.45.

20 Ibid., p.36.

21 Netflix, 2009. Reference guide on our freedom and responsibility culture.

22 Hytner, R., 2013. Interviewed by Greg Orme at Saatchi & Saatchi, London, 26 September.

23 Catliff, N., 2013. Nick Catliff, managing director at Lion TV, interviewed by Greg Orme on 21 May.

24 Zander, B. and Stone Zander, R., 2000. *The art of possibility.* Boston, MA: Harvard Business School Press.

25 Amabile, T.M. and Khaire, M., 2008. Creativity and the role of the leader. *Harvard Business Review*, October. Available at: <http://hbr. org/2008/10/creativity-and-the-role-of-the-leader/ar/1>.

26 Ibid.

27 Isaacson, W., 2012. The real leadership lessons from Steve Jobs. *Harvard Business Review*, April 2012.

28 Collins, J. and Porras, J.I., 2000. *Built to last: successful habits of visionary companies*. London: Random House Business Books. p.43–5. The authors talk about the 'No Tyranny of the Or (Embrace the Genius of The And)'. The Yin and Yang symbol is used throughout the book rejecting (p.43) 'the rational view that cannot easily accept paradox'.

Habit 4 Become a talent impresario

1 Afshar, V., 2013. 100 Tweetable Business Culture Quotes from Brilliant Executives [online]. Available at: <www.huffingtonpost. com/vala-afshar/100-tweetable-business-cu_b_3575595.html>.

2 Chin, P., CEO Langland, 2013. Interviewed by Greg Orme, 6 September.

3 Langland, 2013. Andrew Spurgeon webpage available at: <http:// beta.langland2013.co.uk/#/people/andrew-spurgeon-creative- director>.

4 Caves, R.E., 2000. *Creative industries: contacts between art and commerce*. Boston, MA: Harvard University Press.

5 Isaacson, W., 2012. The real leadership lessons from Steve Jobs. *Harvard Business Review*, April.

6 Ibid.

7 *London Evening Standard*, 2013. Dyson to hire 650 skilled workers. *London Evening Standard*, [online]. Available at: <www.standard. co.uk/business/business-news/dyson-to-hire-650-skilled- workers-8799129.html>. 5 September.

8 Quote and insight from Sutton, R.I., 2001.The weird rules of creativity. *Harvard Business Review*, September. p.96.

9 See the Dyson website. Available at: <www.careers.dyson.com>.

10 Gratton, L., 2007. *Hot spots: why some companies buzz with energy and innovation – and others don't*. Harlow: Financial Times Prentice Hall. p.56

11 Amabile, T.M., 1998. How to kill creativity. *Harvard Business Review*, September.

12 A debt of thanks here to Professor Teresa M. Amabile whose model this is developed from, Gordon Torr who I saw looks at the overlaps in this way and Professor John Bates who sent me his thinking on the same area.

13 Pink, D.H. 2009. *Drive: the surprising truth about what motivates us.* Edinburgh: Cannongate Books.

14 Ibid, p. 46.

15 Gratton, L., 2007. *Hot spots: why some companies buzz with energy and innovation – and others don't.* Harlow: Financial Times Prentice Hall. p.56.

16 Capodagli, B. and Jackson, L., 2009. *Innovate the Pixar way: business lessons from the world's most creative corporate playground.* McGraw-Hill Professional. p.54.

17 Gratton, L., 2007. *Hot spots: why some companies buzz with energy and innovation – and others don't.* Harlow: Financial Times Prentice Hall. p.56.

18 Ibarra, H. and Hansen, M.T., 2011. Are you a collaborative leader? *Harvard Business Review,* July. p.73.

19 Figures from Hay Group. The employee turnover threat to your organization. The Hay Group [online]. Available at: <http://web. haygroup.com/0-the-employee-turnover-threat-to-your-organizat ion?gclid=CLaymrqGzboCFQjKtAodLnwA8Q>.

20 In 2011 the Corporate Executive Board's quarterly study of 20,000 employees over the second half of 2011 took a look at the biggest driver of employee retention work through attraction, hiring, retention, development.

21 Casserly, M., 2011. What employees want more than a raise in 2012. Forbes 2011 [online]. Available at: <www.forbes.com/sites/ meghancasserly/2011/12/15/what-employees-want-more-than-a-raise-in-2012/>.

22 Figures from Hay Group. The employee turnover threat to your organization. The Hay Group [online]. Available at: <http://web. haygroup.com/0-the-employee-turnover-threat-to-your-organizat ion?gclid=CLaymrqGzboCFQjKtAodLnwA8Q>.

23 McCord, P., 2014. How Netflix reinvented HR. *Harvard Business Review,* January–February.

24 Ibid.

Habit 5 Know *why* you do what you do

1 Afshar, V., 2013. 100 Tweetable Business Culture Quotes from Brilliant Executives [online]. Available at: <www.huffingtonpost. com/vala-afshar/100-tweetable-business-cu_b_3575595.html>.

2 Conway, E., 2009. IMF puts total cost of crisis at £7.1 trillion. *Telegraph* [online]. Available at: <www.telegraph.co.uk/finance/newsbysector/banksandfinance/5995810/IMF-puts-total-cost-of-crisis-at-7.1-trillion.html>. 8 August.

3 Barclays Transform Programme. Barclays purpose and values' [PDF]. Available at: <http://group.barclays.com/about-barclays/about-us/transform/values>.

4 From a quote by Nilofer Merchant, Silicon Valley CEO and author.

5 Isaacson, W., 2012. The real leadership lessons from Steve Jobs. *Harvard Business Review*, April.

6 BBH staff booklet. Some things that matter to us. Bartle Bogle Hegarty.

Habit 6 Connect through shared values

1 Ogilvy & Mather, 2013. Tham Khai Meng on innovation: pervasive creativity. Available at: <www.ogilvy.com/On-Our-Minds/Articles/Jan-2013-Innovation-Pervasive-Creativity.aspx.>

2 Broadbent, T., 2012. The Ogilvy & Mather guide to effectiveness. Ogilvy & Mather.

3 Ogilvy & Mather , 2013. Ogilvy & Mather retains network of the year title at Cannes Lions 2013. Ogilvy & Mather [online]. Available at: <www.ogilvy.com/News/Press-Releases/June-2013-OM-Retains-Network-of-the-Year-Title-at-Cannes-Lions-2013.aspx>.

4 Afshar, V., 2013. 100 Tweetable Business Culture Quotes from Brilliant Executives [online]. Available at: <www.huffingtonpost.com/vala-afshar/100-tweetable-business-cu_b_3575595.html>.

5 Arguably the only exceptions are the armed forces and emergency services, which require their personnel to lay their life on the line in the line of duty.

6 Murphy, S., 2013. Interviewed by Greg Orme at Sky Grant Way, Isleworth, 29 August.

7 Collins, J. and Porras, J.I., 2000. *Built to last: successful habits of visionary companies*. London: Random House Business Books.

8 Scarlett, K. What is employee engagement? Scarlett Surveys International [online]. Available at: <www.scarlettsurveys.com/papers-and-studies/white-papers/what-is-employee-engagement>.

9 Gallup, 2007 cited in Rayton, B., Dodge, T. and D'Analeze, T., 2012. The evidence: employment engagement task force "nailing the evidence" workgroup. Engage for Success. 12 November.

10 Hakanen, 2008 cited in Rayton, B., Dodge, T. and D'Analeze, T., 2012. The evidence: employment engagement task force "nailing the evidence" workgroup. Engage for Success. 12 November.

11 CBI Harvey Nash Employment Survey, 2012, cited in Rayton, B., Dodge, T. and D'Analeze, T., 2012. The evidence: employment engagement task force "nailing the evidence" workgroup. Engage for Success. 12 November.

12 The Hay Group, 2010 cited in Rayton, B., Dodge, T. and D'Analeze, T., 2012. The evidence: employment engagement task force "nailing the evidence" workgroup. Engage for Success. 12 November.

13 Based on Campbell, A., 1996. *The Ashridge mission model, mission and management commitment.* Ashridge Strategic Management Centre. I have added the concept of culture into the model (as well as behavioural standards) as I found it to be language of my clients and a useful way to make the intangible 'climate' of a business something that can be influenced and managed.

14 This story was used in Netflix, 2009. Reference guide on our freedom and responsibility culture. p.6.

15 Referenced in MacLeod, D. and Clarke, N., 2008. The four drivers of engagement in the UK government. *Macleod Review* as 'organisational integrity'.

16 Netflix, 2009. Reference guide on our freedom and responsibility culture. pp.10–18.

17 With thanks to the inspiring Brian Bacon of the Oxford Leadership Academy.

18 The answer is Disney.

19 Poulter, S., 2013. Tesco profits cut by half after US failure: American stores will be sold or closed and UK openings scaled back as supermarket reels from £2 billion blow. *Mail Online* [online]. 17 April 2013. Available at: <www.dailymail.co.uk/news/article-2310315/Tesco-profits-cut-half-US-failure-American-stores-sold-closed-UK-openings-scaled-supermarket-reels-2billion-blow.html#ixzz2XQcmjP54>. 17 April.

20 Goodwin, C., 2009. Fresh & Easy: Tesco's great American disaster. *The Week* [online]. Available at: <www.theweek.co.uk/politics/23805/fresh-easy-tescos-great-american-disaster.> 27 April

21 Poulter, S., 2013. Tesco profits cut by half after US failure: American stores will be sold or closed and UK openings scaled back as supermarket reels from £2 billion blow. *Mail Online* [online]. 17 April 2013. Available at: <www.dailymail.co.uk/news/article-2310315/Tesco-profits-cut-half-US-failure-American-stores-sold-closed-UK-openings-scaled-supermarket-reels-2billion-blow.html#ixzz2XQcmjP54>. 17 April.

22 Hemp, P. and Stewart, T.A., 2004. Leading change when business is good: an interview with Samuel J. Palmisano. *Harvard Business Review*, December. Available at: <http://hbr.org/2004/12/leading-change-when-business-is-good/ar/1>.

23 Indebted for some of these great questions to Osterwalder, A. and Pigneur, Y., 2010. *Business model generation*, Hoboken, NJ: John Wiley & Sons.

Habit 7 Build a business playground

1 Afshar, V., 2013. 100 Tweetable Business Culture Quotes from Brilliant Executives [online]. Available at: <www.huffingtonpost.com/vala-afshar/100-tweetable-business-cu_b_3575595.html>.

2 BSkyB Corporate, 2014. About Sky. Available at: <http://corporate.sky.com/about_sky/our_board_and_management/executive_team>.

3 World of CEOs. Available at: www.worldofceos.com/dossiers/jeremy-darroch>.

4 Murphy, S., 2013. Interviewed by Greg Orme at Sky Grant Way, Isleworth on 29 August.

5 Darran, L., 2013. Interviewed by Greg Orme at Sky on 25 September.

6 It was a remark by the business guru Peter Drucker and subsequently popularised in 2006 by Mark Fields, president of Ford Motor Company. That quote allegedly hangs in the company's War Room.

7 Hegarty, J., 2013. Interviewed by Greg Orme at BBH London on 24 June.

8 Fast Company, 2013. How SAS became the world's best place to work. Fast Company, 25 January.

9 This great list is from Dunlop, J. Top 20 most awesome company offices. Available at: <www.incomediary.com/top-20-most-awesome-company-offices.>

10 See Googlepex Wikipedia entry at: <http://en.wikipedia.org/wiki/Googleplex#Facilities_and_history>.

Habit 8 Balance focus with freedom

1 McCord, P., 2014. How Netflix reinvented HR. *Harvard Business Review*, January–February.

2 Rebuck, G., 2013. Interviewed by Greg Orme on 7 November.

3 Catliff, N., 2013 Interviewed by Greg Orme on 21 May.

4 Stone, B., 2011. Steve Jobs: the return, 1997–2011. *Bloomberg Business Week* [online]. Available at: <http://www.businessweek.com/magazine/the-return-19972011-10062011.html>. 6 October.

5 Isaacson, W., 2012. The real leadership lessons from Steve Jobs. *Harvard Business Review*, April.

6 Torr, G., 2008. *Managing creative people: lessons for leadership in the ideas economy*. Chichester: John Wiley & Sons.

7 David (Michelangelo) Wikipedia entry available at: <http://en.wikipedia.org/wiki/David_(Michelangelo).>

8 Torr, G., 2008. *Managing creative people: lessons for leadership in the ideas economy*. Chichester: John Wiley & Sons. p.253.

9 Ogilvy & Mather. Corporate Culture. Available at: <www.ogilvy.com/About/Our-History/Corporate-Culture.aspx.>

10 Pink, D.H., 2009. *Drive: the surprising truth about what motivates us*. Edinburgh: Cannongate Books. p.95.

11 *The Economist*, 2012. The roots of creativity: throwing muses. *The Economist* [online]. 17 March.

12 3M website. Available at: <www.3m.com>. See also: <http://money.cnn.com/magazines/fortune/most-admired/2013/snapshots/284.html>.

13 Pink, D.H., 2009. *Drive: the surprising truth about what motivates us*. Edinburgh: Cannongate Books. p.95.

14 A claim made by Intuit co-founder Scott Cook in Amabile, T.M. and Khaire, M., 2008. Creativity and the role of the leader. *Harvard Business Review*, October. Available at: <http://hbr.org/2008/10/creativity-and-the-role-of-the-leader/ar/1>.

15 Bell, K., 2012. Lighter, stronger, Gorilla Glass 2 coming soon to your iOS devices. Cult of Mac [online] 2012. Available at: <www.cultofmac.com/138304/lighter-stronger-gorilla-glass-2-coming-soon-to-your-ios-devices/>. .6 January.

16 Sutton, R.I., 2001. The weird rules of creativity. *Harvard Business Review.* September. p. 96.

17 Amabile, T.M. and Khaire, M., 2008. Creativity and the role of the leader. *Harvard Business Review*, October. Available at: <http://hbr.org/2008/10/creativity-and-the-role-of-the-leader/ar/1>.

18 Ibid.

19 Atlassian website available at: www.atlassian.com/company

20 Amabile, T.M. and Khaire, M., 2008. Creativity and the role of the leader. *Harvard Business Review*, October. Available at: <http://hbr.org/2008/10/creativity-and-the-role-of-the-leader/ar/1>., p. 7. A convincing analysis was put forward by Henry Sauermann, then a doctoral candidate at Duke University (now at Georgia Tech), who presented new research carried out in collaboration with Duke Professor Wesley Cohen.

21 Pink, D.H., 2009. *Drive: the surprising truth about what motivates us.* Edinburgh: Cannongate Books. p.93.

22 *Woody Allen: a documentary*, Part 2 [TV programme], BBC, 2013.

23 The names have been changed.

Habit 9 Demolish idea barriers

1 The Producers Alliance for Cinema and Television (PACT) is the trade association representing the commercial interests of UK independent television, film, digital, children's and animation media companies. PACT has a membership of around 450; Channel 4's director of creative diversity, Stuart Cosgrove, said that in 2012–13 Channel 4 worked with 430 suppliers.

2 Cosgrove, S., 2013. Stuart Cosgrove, Channel 4's director of diversity, interviewed by Greg Orme on 1 October.

3 Rebuck, G., 2013. Interviewed by Greg Orme on 7 November.

4 Greiner, L.E., 1972. Evolution and revolution as organizations grow. *Harvard Business Review,* vol. 50(4).

5 Inspired by Netflix, 2009. Reference guide on our freedom and responsibility culture.

6 Lehrer, J., 2012. *Imagine: how creativity works*. New York, NY: Houghton Mifflin Harcourt. p.209.

7 Ibid.

8 WPP. WPP at a glance. Available at: <www.wpp.com/wpp/about/wppataglance/>.

9 Sawyer, K., 2007. *Group genius: the creative power of collaboration*. New York, NY: Basic Books. p.154.

10 In an interview with *The New York Times*.

11 Isaacson, W., 2012. The real leadership lessons from Steve Jobs. *Harvard Business Review*, April.

12 Sheep are important to BBH, as it sees itself as a black sheep standing out from a herd of white ones.

13 Sawyer, K., 2007. *Group genius: the creative power of collaboration*. New York, NY: Basic Books. p.165.

14 Netflix, 2009. Reference guide on our freedom and responsibility culture.

15 Darran, L., 2013. Interviewed by Greg Orme at Sky on 25 September.

16 Shaw, J., 2013. Interviewed by Greg Orme at Digitas Kitcatt Nohr, April 16.

17 Olins, W., 2013. Interviewed by Greg Orme at Saffron HQ in London on May 22.

18 von Hippel, E.A., 1976. The dominant role of users in the scientific instrument innovation process. *Research Policy*, July, 5, no. 3.

19 Kitcatt, P., 2013. Interviewed by Greg Orme at Digitas Kitcatt Nohr on October 1.

20 Traitler, H. and Sam Saguy, I., 2009. Creating successful innovation partnerships. See: <www.ift.org>.

21 Bell, D.E. and Shellman, M., 2009. *Nestlé in 2008*. Harvard Business School.

22 Bell, D.E. and Shellman, M., 2009. *Nestlé in 2008*. Harvard Business School.

23 Lehrer, J., 2012. *Imagine: how creativity works*. New York, NY: Houghton Mifflin Harcourt. p. xv.

24 Goffin, K. and Koners, U., 2011. Tacit knowledge, lessons learnt, and new product development. *Journal of Product Innovation Management*. 28, pp. 300–318.

25 Lehrer, J., 2012. *Imagine: how creativity works*. New York, NY: Houghton Mifflin Harcourt. p.205.

Habit 10 Encourage collisions

1 Nordberg, M., 2013. Former resource coordinator of the Atlas Experiment, CERN, interviewed by Greg Orme on 4 December.

2 Scientific Information Service. Available at: <http://library.web. cern.ch>.

3 Pink, D.H., 2009. *Drive: the surprising truth about what motivates us*. Edinburgh: Cannongate Books. p.22.

4 Gratton, L., 2007. *Hot spots: why some companies buzz with energy and innovation – and others don't*. Harlow: Financial Times Prentice Hall.

5 Afshar, V., 2013. 100 Tweetable Business Culture Quotes from Brilliant Executives [online]. Available at: <www.huffingtonpost. com/vala-afshar/100-tweetable-business-cu_b_3575595.html>.

6 Sproxton, D., 2013. Interviewed by Greg Orme on 3 June.

7 Ogilvy & Mather, 2009. *The eternal pursuit of unhappiness: being very good is no good, you have to be very, very, very, very, very good*. Ogilvy & Mather Worldwide. p.43.

8 Deans, J., 2002. Dyke shows BBC 'yellow card'. *The Guardian* [online]. Available at: <www.theguardian.com/media/2002/ feb/07/broadcasting.bbc>. 7 February.

9 The Founder's Constitution, Article 1, Section 8, Clause 8. Thomas Jefferson to Isaac McPherson, 13 August 1813. Available at: <http://press-pubs.uchicago.edu/founders/documents/ a1_8_8s12.html.>

10 Lehrer, J., 2012. *Imagine: how creativity works*. New York, NY: Houghton Mifflin Harcourt. p.222.

11 Senge, P., 2006. *The fifth discipline: the art and practice of the learning organisation*. London: Random House Business Books.

12 Sawyer, K., 2007. *Group genius: the creative power of collaboration*. New York, NY: Basic Books. p.163.

13 Stenger, W., 2013. As Microsoft buys Nokia, Finns mourn their claim to fame. *The Guardian* [online]. Available at: <www. theguardian.com/world/2013/sep/06/microsoft-nokia-finns-mourn-fame.> 6 September.

14 Bailey, M., 2013. Nokia knocked out: it's three mistakes and the three lessons for brands. BRW [online]. Available at: <www.brw.com.au/p/tech-gadgets/nokia_knocked_brands_for_three_mistakes_mqpBWexoTt192wMmS0OWxJ>. 4 September.

15 Lehrer, J., 2012. *Imagine: how creativity works*. New York, NY: Houghton Mifflin Harcourt. p.143.

16 Ibarra, H. and Hansen, M.T., 2011. Are you a collaborative leader? *Harvard Business Review*, July.

17 Amabile, T., Fisher, C. and Pillemer, J., 2014. IDEO's Culture of Helping. *Harvard Business Review*, January–February.

18 Gratton, L., 2007. *Hot spots: why some companies buzz with energy and innovation – and others don't*. Harlow: Financial Times Prentice Hall. p.43.

19 Ibarra, H. and Hansen, M.T., 2011. Are you a collaborative leader? *Harvard Business Review*, July.

20 Sawyer, K., 2007. *Group genius: the creative power of collaboration*. New York, NY: Basic Books. p.154.

Ten creative business myths debunked

1 These are taken from: Harvard Business Essentials, 2003. Creativity and creative groups in *Managing creativity and innovation: practical strategies to encourage creativity*. Boston, MA: Harvard Business Press. p.80.

2 Hytner, R., 2013. Interviewed by Greg Orme at Saatchi & Saatchi, London, 26 September.

3 Bilton, C., 2007. *Management and creativity*. Oxford: Blackwell Publishing. p.14.

4 Gladwell, M., 2008. *Outliers: the story of success*. London: Penguin.

5 BBC, Test the Nation 2006. Available at: <www.bbc.co.uk/testthenation/iq_norms.shtml>.

6 The Simpson family first appeared as 'The Simpsons shorts' (a series of 48 one-minute shorts) in *The Tracey Ullman Show* on 19 April 1987.

Index

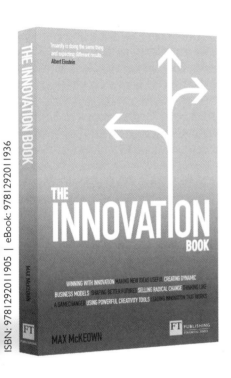
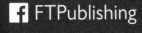